In this new popular version of the successful *Ceremony of Innocence*, Kay Carmichael looks at the way we deal with feelings in private, in personal relationships, in the family, in the workplace, in everyday life.

In a world where children are encouraged not to cry and adults turn off from chaos and disasters we feel we can't influence, it seems all the more relevant.

Central to all survival and creativity is being able to feel . . . and express feelings. Tears are an important symbol of our humanity. Yet to get people to act without passion for hurt or injustice, they have to be told that tears are stupid. The dramatic consequences of this for people are ably and convincingly demonstrated . . . for children, for parents, for teachers and carers, in relationships, in organisations and in the political management of our responses to events.

This challenging and compelling book is, of course, a "good weepy". And importantly, it points a way back to respect for the emotions.

Kay Carmichael is a well-known writer and broadcaster. She has been a social policy adviser to government and has wide experience in psychiatry, social work, child guidance and prisons. She has spent much of her time concerned with children, poverty, women's issues and minority groups.

FOR CRYING OUT LOUD! is a newly written version of Kay Carmichael's *Ceremony of Innocence—tears, power and protest*.

What they've said about it . . .

" An inspiring book. Required reading for anyone who has ever felt ashamed of crying."

Emma Thompson

"Weep and you weep alone—is no longer true. Read this book and you'll be in great company."

Mavis Nicholson

" . . . original and compelling . . . takes us from the innermost recesses of our being to the struggle for justice."

Lesley Macdonald *Coracle*

"So superb a book . . ."

Donald MacDonald *West Highland Free Press*

"Looks with frightening clarity at how we deny human compassion."

Maureen Oswin *Community Care*

"A book that educates the emotions . . . how subversive! Great!"

Derek Rodger *Scottish Child*

"Leading self-evident truths blister up on the pages of this extraordinary book like tears. . . till finally, gloriously, she outlines a possibility of personal and collective change."

Janice Galloway *Scotland on Sunday*

"Kay Carmichael emphasises throughout that the ability to be able to feel for yourself and your own vulnerability is essential for the capacity to feel for others."

Jean Hardy *The Friend*

"Does not fall easily into any pigeonhole . . . it has enormous validity, is dramatic, well written . . . Above all it is an interesting read."

Cary Cooper *Times Literary Supplement*

for *crying* out loud!

previous books by the author

Ceremony of Innocence
Macmillan, 1991

for *crying* out loud!

Kay Carmichael

Argyll publishing

First published in 1993 by
Argyll Publishing
Glendaruel
Argyll
PA22 3AE

Acknowledgements are due to The Macmillan Press Ltd for permission to publish material in this book that appeared originally in *Ceremony of Innocence—tears, power and protest* (1991).

British Libary Cataloguing-in-Publication Data.
A catalogue record for this book is available from the British Library.

ISBN 1 874640 30 0

Typeset and Linotronic output by
Cordfall, Civic Street, Glasgow
Printed and bound in Great Britain by
HarperCollins, Glasgow

for
a more loving world

Circular as our way
is, it leads not back to that snake-haunted
garden, but onward to the tall city
of glass that is the laboratory of the spirit.

R S Thomas

Acknowledgements

This book has been written with the help of many men and women who have shared with me their struggle to move from personal distress to self healing. Their courage has been a constant illumination to me. My guides in the process have been Dr Cameron Macdonald in his understanding of the inner life and Mrs Elinor Goldschmied who has so generously, over many years, shared with me her unique knowledge of child development and group process. I am also grateful to my publisher and editor Derek Rodger for his unstinting help. Finally my thanks and my love go to my grandchildren, Victoria and Christopher, for everything I have learned from watching them grow in such creative ways.

Kay Carmichael
Argyll, April 1993

Contents

chapter one
Starting point

The little girl was standing by herself outside the security guard's hut. She was weeping bitterly. She looked to be about three years old. Her nose was running, her mouth was open, deep sobs racked her body. And no one took the slightest notice of her.

She was a scrap of humanity in deepest misery and as far as the adults in her environment were concerned, she might as well not have existed. Yet her whole self was in despair and no one in the dismal former army barracks moved towards her. It was a massive four-storey, grey, rectangular building cut off from the bustling city of Hong Kong by a fence topped with barbed wire and divided along its length by fetid drains. Many Vietnamese families lived here in these primitive conditions, waiting patiently if hopelessly for the chance to enter other countries to work and make new lives for themselves and their children. There were few adults about and like the little girl, only a few aimless children.

I found this little girl's pain intolerable. I moved towards her and asked our guide to this refugee camp to explain why she was crying. At this point she was picked up and rushed off, still wailing.

That night I woke up weeping. I was crying for myself and not for the little girl. I had somehow known looking at her, exactly what she was feeling. The difference in our ages, skin colour, shape of eyes, language—all these were irrelevant. We seemed to be two creatures linked by a special kind of pain—the pain of the uncomforted child.

In any High Street or shopping mall where a child has been left in her pram and wakened to find herself alone surrounded by strange images, you can see the face of terror. It is flushed and contorted into an expression of agony and if allowed to go on, the screaming becomes choked and hysterical. Children can look and sound as if they are in the third layer of hell. If an adult stood in the street and screamed with that degree of terror everyone would be halted in their tracks and a doctor or ambulance called for. But when a baby screams in distress, most people don't even notice.

One or two experiences like this are not going to damage a fundamentally healthy relationship between a child and its world. But a steady diet of experience that teaches that you cannot command care and relief from distress, that the adult is not there for you, wears away all the confidence in the world.

We all carry our own memories of tears—tears of panic, tears of terror, tears of anxiety, grief or betrayal. So in adult life, the things that move us to tears are different. Different things have the power over us.

My house could burn down and I would walk away without a tear. But if I stumble and fall in the street, I have to fight back floods. As in the case of most people, a complex story lies behind my fear of helplessness and having no one to comfort me. I used to think there was a child within me, crying all the time.

For various family reasons I was sent as a very young child, to the convent of St Joseph of Cluny in Ayrshire. All the nuns had to be called "Mother", with the exception of the Reverend Mother, a charming but remote figure. I had no idea where my own mother had disappeared to when she left me there. One of the nuns, Mother Stanislaus took a particular interest in me and whenever visitors were being shown round the school, I would be sent for. She would stand me in front of her and say to the visitors, "Watch this". As she held her forefinger up in front of my nose, like a performing monkey in a circus act, I would burst into tears. I can still remember how I used to try so hard not to do what she wanted but always the tears and the misery overflowed. And I have often wondered since what it was about me that fueled her sadism.

For many people, childhood is a nightmare from which they never recover. Children are constantly betrayed. Sometimes dramatically by being left abandoned. More often in much simpler ways. Children are lied to, bullied, roughly handled as they are dressed and undressed, shouted at and shaken. And all this is done by people the child loves with every fibre of her body.

So it is not surprising later in life that betrayal is a recurring theme for many people. A sense of betrayal evokes tears that are often mixed with anger and the desire for revenge. Being beaten by someone you love is an act of betrayal which makes the beaten child—from Adolf Hitler to the abused or neglected child next door—stalk the world seeking revenge.

The deepest sense of betrayal does not inspire revenge but withdrawal. The desire for revenge does seem to indicate a continuing link with the one who has betrayed you and sometimes the pain is too great for that.

The key to heal the wounds of betrayal lies in the ability to comfort the child. My experience, and the experience of many other people, of being comforted while crying, is not a happy one. As adults we are very unsure about accepting comfort. Maybe it was not given to us when we needed it. Maybe it was given erratically or with conditions.

For myself I prefer to go off like a wounded animal and cry alone. Just see myself through the distress. I have learned from some people that it doesn't need to be like that but still find it hard to believe. Being able to comfort each other is very important. Lucky children learn it from their mother or father. But some parents have never been comforted themselves and don't know how to offer it to their own children. My memory of my own mother was that she could not comfort me. It seemed that whatever was happening to me was never as bad as what was happening to her. But my grandmother comforted me and from her I learnt enough to console my mother. And then in the course of time comfort my own child too. But we can only give to others what we were given ourselves.

Just as when very young we encounter feelings of betrayal and how to cope, it is in early childhood that we first learn if we have permission to protest against pain and injustice. If we secured even a modest acceptance of our feelings, we have a chance. Even if for whatever reason a child's parents can't manage to give acceptance, she can be lucky and have a grannie or grandad who gives bits of loving to keep alive energy, courage and hope. She can find a friend or a teacher who treats her as if she were a bit special and reinforces tiny bits of self-esteem—someone who can see past the defences and love, nurture and heal the hurt. She may through a variety of life experiences find the core of pain, transform it and find hope.

We can also take our pain into the world and ask those who also suffer whatever hardship or injustice to join us in transforming it. The very act of sharing pain, of weeping together, can so often bring a shift of energy.

So this book is an attempt to share my own experience of pain and joy and all the emotions in between with the reader. When so much else in the way our world is constructed seems to work to bury and deny feelings and dry our tears, my hope is that you will be enabled to get in contact with your own. And in knowing and sharing our deepest insights, the whole point is to release the energies that change and improve our world.

It's probably no surprise that the little Vietnamese girl in the Hong Kong camp was left to cry uncomforted. Her parents, living in their crowded cages had maybe little to offer. While we can understand her parents' problems, while we may even forgive them their neglect, can we forgive ourselves when we turn our heads away from their suffering and collude with the conditions which create that camp and all the other camps in the world, with and without fences, through which children wander uncomforted?

chapter two
Floods of tears

What our civilisation needs today . . . is the cultivation of an exquisite sensitivity and an incomparable tenderness . . . Unnameable horrors have paraded before us and worse evils threaten because we have been unable to wipe the blank stare of indifference from our stony tearless faces.

Lewis Mumford *The Conduct of Life*

We cry from infancy to death. We sing about tears. People write songs and poems about them. In the BBC Glasgow music library I found over two hundred songs listed with "tears" or "crying" in the title. Talking to people in groups and workshops, they poured out their thoughts and feelings about why they cried, where they cried, when they cried.

Crying and weeping have been used by humans of all ages, all races, creeds, and in all societies to express their deepest feelings. There are numerous references to tears in the Bible, in the Koran, the Hindu Upanishads and in every nation's folklore. The salt water used in the Jewish ceremony of Seder represents the tears that were shed by the Israelites when they were slaves in Egypt.

Rain has been widely referred to as if it were tears from god, or the sky weeping in compassion for the sorrows of those of us on earth. In stories from every country and every race of people, we find references to tears—tears of grief, tears of anger, tears of joy. Fairy tales from all cultures tell of the magic of tears.

At first I thought tears were only important to women. I was wrong. I discovered that given the chance, many men were as eager to talk about their tears and how they cry. Also why they don't. I should have known. My childhood memories are full of images of drunk Glasgow men weaving their way home from the pub on a Saturday night, singing weepy, nostalgic songs. And if they found a shoulder to lean on would cry noisily and pathetically. Many of the men I spoke to about crying said their only release was at the cinema, at the theatre, or while watching t.v. What men seemed to fear most was that their tears would be laughed at or they would be seen as weak. Some men expressed a sense of anger that women have so much more freedom to express feelings. They didn't realise that there are also women whose lives have been pervaded with a sense of shame whenever they have been forced into tears.

Our attitude to crying and tears is built into us, like so much else at a very early age, first by our parents, and later by teachers, employers and any figures of authority that we encounter. Friends, exposed to the same influences, share feelings of when and why you can and can't cry. To help me understand the whole process, I began to draw on my own experiences and memories—always a painful task that never seems to get easier! I tried to remember too, the life stories of those whose path in life I have shared—friends, associates, those I have worked with. I reread the Bible, that most marvellous source of human experience and I found the Old Testament brimming over with references to tears, weeping and crying. The texts of other religions are the same.

I realised that we cry from infancy to death but understand practically nothing about the process. But the invisible subject was gradually becoming visible.

I began to sense that the part tears and crying play in childhood and the way we deal with the world through them is important for establishing healthy caring personal relationships. But even more than that, tears are an important symbol of our humanity—a touchstone of our capacity to feel hurt for our own sakes but also to feel hurt for others. So the extent to which we are able to feel for others is a measure of how democratic we are as a society. Democratic relationships are nothing if they are not compassionate.

Tears and crying arise from emotional responses to our deepest consciousness of being human. It seems to me that there are three primary sources of the awareness of our humanity. It is from these sources that our tears must originally spring.

The most powerful of these is the sense of **our own mortality**. We know that all things have a transient fleeting nature, particularly our own lives. Virgil spoke of these tears:

> ". . . and mortality her tears.
> The woes of man touch the heart."

We all have to come to terms with our physical vulnerability as we walk erect through the world carrying everything that makes us function inside a fragile skull balanced on a tube down our spine, with the knowledge that our death is inevitable.

The second source is our **need for other people**. No matter how much we aspire to be independent, we are all from birth linked into relationships. These may be good. They may be bad. Their success or failure will be the greatest source of suffering or joy we are capable of experiencing. There is no pain greater than the loss of love. Sharper than the serpent's tooth is the ingratitude of a child or a lover for the intensely focussed passion we have lavished on them. Equally there is no greater joy than the mutual love between adults, or between parents and children.

The third aspect of being human that is a source of suffering and joy and the source spring of tears lies in our struggle as individuals and in groups to **change our world**. The world is physically turbulent and dangerous. Politically it is volatile. We suffer in our struggle to change and improve it. Unlike other creatures, we have not been content to accept the fate that nature has decreed for us. We have challenged the gods and from that has developed many marvels of creativity, heroism and imagination. The contradiction is that somewhere buried in those capacities we carry a willingness to inflict pain and death on our own kind. It is the shadow that lies over all of us. None can be free until we recognise it in ourselves.

To begin to think about these deep kinds of questions is to think about being human. And inevitably being aware of our own mortality, our vulnerability to emotions in relationships, and all the pain and suffering involved in changing the world however modestly, puts us in touch with the sum of human suffering. And questions like, what does it all mean?

Religions of one sort or another try to offer answers and explanations for the terrifying irrationality of these ills that afflict us. There is no religious leader who does not find it necessary to offer an explanation for physical, emotional and spiritual pain. Some of these religious explanations down through human history have been bizarre. Others have been majestic. But there is a constant surge of human need to have the question of personal suffering given dignity through understanding and ritual. Tears have played an important part in this process.

In the western world, our mainly secular society has affected views of what religion has to offer. Much of the institutional church has been rejected but many people have retained the rituals of baptism, marriage and funerals and recognise their deep significance. Birth and death are sacramental experiences that seem to demand public as well as a private notice. Rituals of baptism, marriage and funerals are times when tears flow . . . tears of joy, pleasure, pride and grief. Even secular societies have to find ways of meeting these primary human responses by acknowledging their meaning.

But if suffering is universal, so too is the human drive to overcome it and seek happiness. It was this realisation that brought me back to tears because time and time again people have said to me, "It was only when I accepted and understood my tears that I began to pull myself out of my despair."

I began to understand that there are different ways of crying. Some tears just leave you more exhausted and despairing. Others leave behind a feeling of coldness and detachment. But some experiences of crying are creative—the tears have a sense of purpose—the person crying is left relaxed and at peace. The emotion that triggered the tears is acknowledged and let go.

Such crying is especially important in bereavement. At a certain stage words cannot be found until tears come. At the inquest into the deaths of the Hungerford massacre victims, the chairman of the bench, speaking in tribute to clerk of the court who was among those killed, said, "I find it impossible to put into words the shock felt in this court on a day like this. Perhaps we all find tears more appropriate." A significant body of work has now built up in psychosomatic medicine to substantiate this intuitive understanding of the importance of tears to well-being.

That's not the whole story of course. Some people dare not cry. It has been forbidden them. Their awareness of suffering has been denied them and thus their capacity to know joy. And this prohibition works on the personal level and in the family, the group and the wider society. A whole sea of expectations surrounds the decision whether to complain or not, whether to comply or dissent. Whether in the everyday experience of complaining that the coffee's cold in a cafe, whether in the life turning events like love and marriage, or in attitudes to political power, the decision to complain, contradict, express disapproval or disgust is often the sum of our personal and social histories.

But it is in the ability to know that we suffer and in the ability to be aware of our joy that we are truly human. In this awareness lies our capacity to shape and plan our lives, to mould our future and the future of the world in which we live. It is from this awareness that we can learn to reduce unnecessary suffering and maximise joy for ourselves. And if we can do it for ourselves, we can help others to do the same.

It is when we cease to be aware, when that awareness has been denied us, when we have denied it, sold it for a mess of pottage or refused to claim it, that our humanity is threatened. Our tears are a fountain of renewal of the capacity to be aware of sorrow and joy on which we can always draw.

chapter three
Stone-age babies; technology-age parents

Each of us, whether born in a high flat in a Glasgow housing scheme, a city penthouse, an affluent suburb, a third world shanty town or a mud hut in the jungle . . . each of us learns the rules of living in that community. Our willingness to obey the rules is taught in lots of little ways every day. But basically we attach ourselves to them and believe in them at some level either through love of or fear of the adults who care for us.

Each of us has been through this process of learning what is considered tolerable and intolerable behaviour. And by and large we hold onto these rules for most of our lives. We shift our attitudes to these basic assumptions about life only when a majority of our fellow citizens shift theirs. And we use roughly the same ways of showing our children how to behave and how not to behave as were used for us.

The economic network in which the family lives is the biggest factor in influencing exactly how this is done. The actual needs of the child are very much secondary. A look at how children are treated in other different societies can be instructive.

Melvin Konner, a distinguished American anthropologist, went to live with the !Kung San society in the Kalahari Desert. Here was a people who lived as hunter gatherers. The simplicity of life made it natural for babies in their first year of life never to be out of their mother's sight, if not her arms. He believes that in highly developed wealthy economies there is no biological advantage for the child to be cared for by one parent as opposed to being cared for equally by two. He sees no biological reason why this marvellous experience should be reserved for women. Indeed, in some countries the idea of both parents taking responsibility for child care is being seen as an ideal to be achieved and paternity leave from work is now being claimed as well as maternity leave.

But the more common pattern is still that the mother (or a female carer if the mother is working) will have the vital early responsibility for baby. The father, if involved at all, will be so in the later stages where the child is more independent, mobile, verbal and capable of feeding itself.

Even so girls will be brought up differently from boys. Girls are more likely to be given the right to weep, to complain, to make a fuss, to declare their pain and unhappiness. Boys will be prepared for the world of competition, material achievement and endurance of suffering. Their distress will be dealt with quite differently.

Konner tells how the !Kung mother and child operate. They live in total interdependence for the first year. The nipple is always available to the baby. His research showed that there was an average of only six seconds between an infant beginning to be fretful and the mother responding. The mother is with the infant twenty-four hours a day—an idea that would fill most mothers in the "advanced" world with horror.

Such a regime is in stark contrast to the highly individualistic society in which many Europeans and North Americans live. Here parents claim their right to space, freedom and privacy even while their child is still a baby. Those who can will return to work in the world of male values and delegate the most intimate tasks of parenting to other young women, most of whom have failed in society's eyes to achieve the job status that would enable them to avoid child care. They will be unlikely to give the intense and devoted attention necessary to sooth baby's worried brow.

Few parents can afford a trained nanny who would expect , in addition to caring for the baby, to have someone else to do the washing, ironing and general cleaning. Untrained carers are usually expected to do all these things as well as care for the baby. It is hardly surprising if baby's distress is ignored or smothered in sugary foods.

When there are two small children the stress on a carer is even greater. Walking invisibly into many a small suburban semi that the mother has left with such a rush in the morning, you find an eighteen year old carrying a baby on one arm, wielding a hoover with the other, followed by a grizzling toddler. Many children will have a six-monthly or yearly succession of these carers, many of whom may still be struggling with their own problems of growing up.

Where the parent has no alternative but to work and use public child care services, it is even less likely that the child will have the individual attention that ensures comfort. Staff in public child care facilities are frequently under stress through sheer pressure of work. And their training seldom equips them to cope with their own responses to tears, crying and distress. Like parents they use their own rough and ready philosophy based on how they themselves were brought up.

In the industrial world, the sound of a child crying—left for example in a pram outside a shop and giving out heart-breaking screams of distress—raises little comment. But in a world of early rising for work, small houses with poor sound insulation, the howl of an infant during the night ceases to be a private matter. In a world uncertain about the nature of caring and the nature of loving, it signals irritation on the part of the neighbours and a sense of failure on the part of the parent.

In adults uncertain of their own capacity to care, the crying baby rouses memories of their own unsatisfied needs. So at the point where the parent may be most vulnerable, tired, unsupported and alone, she is faced with a choice—either to repeat with the child the same techniques that were used by her own parents of hitting or frightening her into silence; or to treat the cry of the child as she herself would have wanted to be treated.

In the !Kung world the sound of crying is hardly an issue in normal everyday life. When it does occur it will mean serious distress and be shown respect within the group. Also there are no memories buried deep within the psyche of unrewarded and neglected screams of distress to be reactivated in the adults of the community. The encounter with the crying child will be uncluttered by the ghosts of one's own pain.

It requires a remarkable degree of insight to break the patterns we were offered by our own parents. If the response to unacceptable behaviour was to be hit, then "It never did me any harm" is another way of saying, "My parents could not do wrong. I must have been bad if they hit me. I must have deserved it." The person who takes that view is unable to separate their own judgement from that of their parents and can only follow docilely in their footsteps.

The implications personally of such a view is that you are likely to lean to the conservative in bringing up your own children. The consequences socially and politically when multiplied across the population are potentially dramatic. Many writers and commentators have said as much. Jean Liedloff who wrote a book called *The Continuum Concept* argued that many personal problems and most social ills are caused by the way we bring up our children in the "advanced" countries. She also lived with a "primitive" tribe and watched how they cared for their infants. She argues that the human embryo is programmed to expect certain responses from the outside world. At birth the earliest expectation is for constant contact with the mother's skin and body for the first months of life, probably until the child is independently mobile, and then for a long time after that when the child feels the need. Deprivation of this experience, Liedloff describes as a kind of torture.

She believes that the vast majority of parents love their children deeply and have no idea of the suffering they are causing or the agony of the baby left alone to weep in its cot. As adults, we seem to need words spoken or written before we take them seriously. Body language has less command over us. But body language is all that a baby has. Babies cannot put their complaints into words. They cannot appeal to higher authority. Even more, they cannot link their pain and distress at being left alone to the cause of it. If not abandoned for too long they greet their parents with joy when they return.

But it is our human capacity for choice that tears us apart from our stone-age babies. If the !Kung tribe that Melvin Konner studied or the Yequana described by Jean Liedloff were suddenly transported to New York or London or Glasgow, in two generations they may have become full members of a consumerist, technological society but they would have abandoned their ways of bringing up their children and have reproduced the same problems that we have.

Our problem is how to help our stone-age babies survive the emotional deprivation of the world we are creating. We can care for our children physically, but how can we preserve their sanity?

Only parents can do that. But parents need the help, the confidence and the support of the whole community. Those whose own children have grown up can reassure younger parents that even the most inconsolably demanding infants will stop squalling in their own good time. With loving acceptance and security that will happen sooner rather than later.

We all need to recognise the anxieties and conflicts facing young parents—their fears about what the neighbours, their mothers-in-law, the other people in the restaurant will say. By helping and supporting them we make life easier for their babies as well. And many of the sources of anxiety are built into our way of life. Shops, hotels, restaurants, trains, buses—all are designed for adults without children. They should be reorganised to honour parents with babies, not discriminate against them. Most of all, each of us needs to honour the infant we once were.

In today's world many young parents are facing intolerable conflicts. I met one young mother changing her baby's nappy in a public washroom. He was gurgling and laughing up at her and I expressed my delight and admiration for this happy baby. To my dismay she burst into tears before she explained that she had only one more week at home with him because she had to go back to work to help pay the mortgage.

Other mothers may choose to go back to work convinced that they will be better and more loving mothers on a part-time basis. Some mothers may prefer to reduce their standard of living and stay home. But wherever babies are cared for we need to be responsive to their emotional as well as their physical needs.

chapter four
Why cry?

Cry-baby-cry
Punch him in the eye
Tie him to a lamp-post
And leave him there to die

Children's rhyme

Crying is primarily a signal. It is the only one of the very few available to a small creature who needs care but who cannot yet talk, crawl, jump up and down, clutch or find any other way of engaging the attention of a responsible adult.

It is interesting that after six weeks of life, crying produces not only noise but tears as well. That lusty sound of crying is the basic way that infants programmed to survive draw attention to the fact that all is not well with them. But what use are those cascades of water that some of us continue to produce for the rest of our lives . . . sometimes to our embarrassment and shame, sometimes to our pleasure and relief?

Infants who can produce tears have a better chance of surviving. Tearless crying, if it goes on for any length of time, can cause the soft, moist lining of the nose and throat to dry up When this happens babies are more vulnerable to infection. So those who survived in the early days of the human race produced children who had this built in genetic advantage. We became a race of weepers, creatures who produce moisture which bathes our eyes—moisture that scientists have discovered is much more complex than anyone could have imagined.

In 1922 Alexander Fleming, the pioneer of penicillin, discovered that tears contain an anti-bacterial enzyme which prevents infection. Every time we blink, this is spread across the eye surface. About sixty tiny glands in the eyelid produce moisture, and when we pick up a bit of grit or any other irritant like cigarette smoke or onion smells, the main lacrimal gland produces a rush of tears to flush out the irritant and so prevent eye damage and restore sight.

In the 1980s we learned that the chemical composition of "emotional" tears—that is tears stemming from feelings like grief—is different from tears stimulated by an irritant to the eye like peeled onions. There is still much to be learned but it is already clear that some of the content of certain kinds of tears belongs to the family of brain chemicals known as endorphines. These are thought to modulate pain sensation and stress-induced changes in the immune system. Tears seem to produce a kind of self-medication which eases states of tension.

Like so many of the normal things that make us function day to day, tears are taken for granted. We cry and weep in the lavatory, in our beds, in the cinema . . . women will weep into the pot of soup they're making. We cry at funerals, we weep at the beauty of a sunset, watching a film on t.v. as the heroine dies or two people who have been separated are reunited.

Crying in response to strong feelings is normally accompanied by other sounds and movements. Although the words crying and weeping tend to be used interchangeably, there are subtle differences between them which express different stages of grief or joy. Crying is more often associated with a noisy attempt to communicate inner feelings like anger or rage or grief at a loss. Weeping usually means the feeling is turned in, the communication is with oneself. Weeping often follows crying. It can imply that the worst has happened and nothing more can be done.

The need to cry does not stop. Life does not stop and the tears go underground. Distress is suffered daily but few things are less common than seeing adults cry. We seem to have to learn codes that enable us to continue to cry, but to do so in ways that will not distress, frighten embarrass or shock other people. We learn to cry like adults.

The signal of distress has to be disguised and given a more acceptable face. The tears are held back, the noise is muted, but the message is unmistakeable.

Sitting in the dentist's chair for example, we cannot weep, scream or shout as we might like to—fingers and instruments are in the mouth and in any case that kind of display is forbidden. We have to be content with the occasional wince or muted moan for which we immediately feel we must apologise. In other situations, some adults produce a brief yelp which would be heartrending if it were prolonged. Even a short yelp may give off an intensity of feeling which makes those around feel anxious. But even this can be covered up with an angry sounding swear word.

Some people learn to bury their tears in their speech. The facial muscles are controlled but the distress is expressed through the tone of voice that never sounds happy or contented. One example is the whiner, always plaintive and self-pitying, but always covering up with a "Look how brave I am" story. Another is the complainer who often begins a sentence in a tone of outrage with, "Have you heard . . ." or "Did you see . . ." The message can be of anger, sometimes well-justified. But the tone is a mixture of anger and distress. It is a controlled tantrum whose real trigger is earlier experiences of injustice that are constantly revived by current events.

In its most creative form, the powerful energy of repressed tears can drive pressure groups and political campaigns. At its worst, it can be a divisive force in organisations—the constant complainer cannot question the conviction on which he has based his life, cannot truly cooperate with anyone or give them hope and courage.

We can weep in distress, rage, even in joy if the intensity of stimulation is high enough. Sometimes the messages can be mixed. I watched an eleven year old girl receiving a television award for the Most Caring Child of the Year because of the way, as an only child whose father is dead, she cares for her severely disabled mother. Seeing her burst into tears, put over by the presenter as "crying for joy", I wondered how much that child was weeping in sorrow for herself. The list of things she did for her mother—taking her to the toilet day and night, washing and dressing her, turning her over in bed—seemed an outrageous imposition. Even though the girl did not recognise it at the time, it must have been exhausting and diminishing of her childhood.

For some people, even sounds which express distress have not been allowed, in the same way that tears have been forbidden. Feeling shows in their faces. In a moment of sudden distress, their expression will take on the classic shape of distress—a turning down of the corners of the mouth, the inner ends of the eyebrows raised so that they lie obliquely over the face, furrows in the forehead. This is the image of grief seen in masks in all cultures throughout the world. One of the most famous is Eduard Munch's painting, *The Scream.* Just as making ourselves smile can in itself give a sensation of cheerfulness, each of us who deliberately puts our face into this shape will make contact with our own sadness.

For some people the classic shape of grief on their faces becomes chronic and habitual. They go around with a frozen cry for all to see. Yet they can be unaware of their own sadness.

There are others who show this expression only when they are alone or not concentrating on a specific task. In company, at work or in conversation, they are lively and animated. Alone or unoccupied, the mask of the frozen cry emerges . . . the schoolchild who daydreams, the secretary in pauses between tasks, the executive sitting in the toilet. It is seen in public places where people may feel alone and anonymous but are surrounded by others. Underground trains and public washrooms provide a perfect setting where the convention is that no one looks at anyone else. It can be especially moving to see women come into the powder room of a restaurant or ballroom where they have been wearing masks of hectic enjoyment and as the door between them and the party swings shut, the mask of gaiety slides off and the frozen cry shows.

But even feeling can be buried underground. When tears and all sounds of crying and all facial signs of distress have been excluded from the life-plan of the adult, the feelings themselves can be denied. The messages which would have been sent to the face and vocal chords are sent to some other set of muscles. Fingers, toes or stomach are clenched. Necks are stiffened, joints tightened and the heart is hardened. Bodies arming themselves against feeling have effects on health that are incalculable.

chapter five
Why not?

Speak roughly to your little boy
And beat him when he sneezes
He only does it to annoy
Because he knows it teases

Lewis Carroll

We can either accept tears and crying or reject them as shameful, humiliating or embarrassing behaviour. The first, accepting them, involves trying to discover the cause of the distress. The second tends to punish and discourage crying in children.

If they are honest, many people are torn between the two and, depending on the pressures of the moment, will comfort or punish. Most parents work out a system for punishing or soothing which fits into their capacity to sympathise and children soon learn to negotiate a maze that may be quite incomprehensible to an outsider. An infant may be allowed to cry but a toddler will be punished. Sympathy may be given to a child who cries because he has fallen and hurt himself, but fury may be aroused if he cries because he has broken something. Crying inside the home may be tolerated but not crying in public. Gentle sobs may be acceptable and howls of rage not, or vice versa. Some parents may be able to accept any form of tears except those that appear to criticise their own behaviour. All of these sometimes inconsistent rules are based on the private individual experience of the parent.

We should never forget how dependent children are on their parent's or other adults' approval, how much they want to please them, how much they will adapt their behaviour to do so. Children will tolerate pain, anxiety and humiliation to secure their parent's love. So it is possible for even the most powerful drive like the need to cry to be muted. Even the feelings that give rise the urge to cry may be driven underground through a whole range of parental messages.

Shaming or ridicule is perhaps the most common. "Big boys don't cry". "Cry baby!" Or the more devastating, "You should be ashamed of making a fool of yourself like that." Messages which shame or ridicule can only be effective of course, when the child is old enough to have some idea of self, and some idea of the kind of person their parent or carer wants them to be. Shame can embed itself deeply into the consciousness of the child, and the associated feelings of guilt will touch and monitor all future behaviour.

Terrorising a child is also a remarkably common form of control. We can watch in shops and supermarkets, at bus stops, in queues. The child is crying at any level from just grizzling to outright howling. The parent is trying to ignore it but the thread breaks and suddenly the child is pounced on, shaken viciously and shouted at or hissed at in the most terrifying way—"Stop it!" with the additional phrase thrown in like, "If you don't stop that crying, I'll really give you something to cry for." Or as I heard one mother say to twins, both of whom were crying, "If you don't stop, I'll give one of you away. Now which will it be?" The child freezes and the crying stops. A resilient child will start again within a few minutes after the shock has worn off when another more effective technique has to be applied.

Pain is the crudest response but, although as morally repulsive as terror, is arguably the least damaging in the long term if it is restricted to a slap. But of course, adults have widely differing levels of self control and the physical punishment can escalate until it becomes cruelty—sometimes even murder. For that reason our society is learning slowly but surely that inflicting physical pain on children, even in the form of "just a slap", can no longer be tolerated. We have no idea how many cases of child abuse have been triggered by crying for comfort that the parent is unable to give. It certainly comes up time after time in court as an offered explanation for cruelty and injury. It is even heard as a defence in child murder. "He just kept on crying and I couldn't stand it any longer." It is as if the adult has become a distressed child himself inside his own head and has had the adult equivalent of a crying tantrum—an explosion of rage—with fatal results.

Blackmail In adults, blackmail is considered one of the more unattractive crimes playing as it does on intimidation and abuse of power. Yet it is constantly used to control children. "You'll make mummy cry if you don't stop crying." "You'll be the death of me with your crying, stop it, I can't stand it." The child is put in touch with her capacity to destroy and made to fear it rather than learn to control it. If she responds honestly to her need to cry, she is told she will damage the person she most loves. It is not a real choice. A false morality is invoked in which the crying child feels "bad" and the non-crying child is a "good" child.

Threats of withdrawal of love are common currency. "Mummy won't love you if you don't stop crying." "I don't like little girls/boys who cry." What horrors are opened up in these sentences—the implication that love is dependent on acceptable behaviour; the notion that love can be switched on and off like a light. What a message to send a little child with into the world of relationships! Or the demonstration of the ultimate withdrawal of love in the appearance of indifference.

A show of indifference to the child's feelings means that no action is taken to comfort or soothe. The parent might turn away, leave the room, or not go to where the child is when the crying starts. The child is allowed to cry itself out, which can last a few minutes or for some hours until the child falls asleep from exhaustion.

Sometimes the indifference is real and not just a show. Recently I watched a commercial creche operating in a gym where mothers left their children while they did aerobics. A seated infant cried unremittingly while the woman in charge laboriously went about a series of routine chores. She seemed immune to the sounds of distress and was puzzled when I intervened. If these messages are constantly repeated the child learns that there is no point asking for help because none will be given. It is interesting that a consistent theme in fairy tales like Cinderella is that tears can be a signal for a rescuer to appear.

Help without sympathy is another device which denies feelings and ignores tears. Busy nursery staff may be tempted to use phrases like, "That's enough of that, let's see what's the matter", as the infant is efficiently checked over, changed and dressed . . . and then left to cry. Other pressures may lead to sympathy being offered without practical help though this response is more likely to be aroused in men who feel helpless when faced with a small child.

As in so many other situations an adult who feels helpless is the most dangerous person a child is likely to encounter. But given help without sympathy or sympathy without help, the child is deprived of the vital learning experience. Feelings and behaviour should go together. Help without sympathy, as some hospital patients asking for a bedpan will tell you, can be experienced as an aggressive act. For children, help without sympathy, duty rather than love, denies the emotional component of the tears and the discomfort that provokes them. This is sometimes put into words like—"Crying won't get you anywhere." "If you keep on crying you'll *never* be able to do anything about it."

Laughter A cheerful, jollying response is common where the parent or carer decides that the cause of distress is trivial. Occasionally this can be a useful and undamaging response. But as a constant way of dealing with distress, pain and fear it really shows a disrespect towards the child's real feelings. And so it leads to shame and ultimately to denial. To be laughed at, rather than with, is not an experience most people enjoy, especially when they are needing comforted.

So if we are forced by the adults in our life to learn that crying is not acceptable, we can—maybe we have to—develop a number of devices or tricks to distract us from our distress. We find something to stop us crying, something that distracts the mind from what is upsetting. The alternative sensation doesn't need to be unpleasant—sucking a thumb, a blanket, later a cigarette. In some countries mothers or nursemaids will stroke a baby boy's genitals to soothe him.

Indeed, masturbation can become a diversion from distress for both girls and boys. Prisons and boarding schools are two settings where the comfort and distraction achieved by masturbation seem much more important than the sexuality. Crying with homesickness can be seen and heard. Rubbing the flesh to distract from the pain can be hidden more easily under the blankets.

Violence can serve the same purpose. Pain and distress is converted to anger either at oneself or at others. Self mutilation, often found among adolescent girls in institutions where they slash themselves with anything sharp, is a seriously misunderstood alternative to weeping.

Other habits may be seen as minor forms of self mutilation or distraction—nose-picking, ear pulling, lip biting, face rubbing, nail biting. Head banging is a common response in children's nurseries where the little ones have learned that crying is a fairly hopeless or unproductive activity. It is a behaviour that has to be given up as the child grows, but its power surely lingers on in the label among young men for the most unhappy and disturbed member of their group—the headbanger!

The essential strategy is to reduce the crying and the fear of crying by substituting something else which, if not positively pleasurable, is at least less painful. The greater the distress the more intense the necessary alternative. Self mutilation by tattoos, drug taking and heavy drinking can be intense. The excitement of stealing reduces the tension for some. Shopping for new clothes helps some women. Many men find the absorption of gambling addictive.

Most of us have learned that if we are under attack, weeping or crying makes us more vulnerable. Women can use this to emphasise their vulnerability, arouse pity and so get themselves out of a pressure situation. Most men are not permitted to use tears in this way. Only when a man has triumphed or accepted an honourable defeat is a show of weakness tolerated. Tears after triumph or defeat in the boxing ring, on the athletic track or the football field may express triumph or relief at survival, or act as a relief from tension. But even here, crying may be seen as a dangerous weakness and a laugh or a joke substituted.

Jewish humour has brought this kind of response to a fine art. Few peoples have had more cause for tears and none have a richer fund of black humour where pain is managed and contained. Two young Jewish women watched their families being led to the gas chamber while they themselves were taken to be stripped and shaved. They told me that on first encountering each other naked and bald, they fell into each other's arms, unable to speak for laughing. The terror and pain were too intolerable to be expressed in any other way.

Law courts provide daily examples of the refusal of young men to admit their emotional vulnerability. They display the bravado of laughter when they may be near to tears. If sentenced to prison, while their mothers may be rending the air with screams of protest, the offenders will smile broadly. The jury, seeing the smile, will take it as an affirmation of villainy. Few will recognise it as a defence against tears which would "unman" them.

chapter six
Crying all my life

"Wake up" said a voice when I was three
"There's a great big world you must go and see"
"Wake up" said a voice when I was eight
"There's a better world you can help create"
"Wake up" said a voice when I was ten
"Or else your egg will be hard again"
"Wake up" said a voice at twenty-nine
"You've a lovely wife called Caroline"
"Wake up" said a voice at fifty four
But the cuckoo was frozen behind its door.

Edward Matchett
Journeys of Nothing in the Land of Everything

In a shop or in the street we watch a toddler being physically hit for crying. Maybe the mother is exhausted trying to cope with an infant as well as a toddler. Or the father is embarrassed at not managing in public. The most obvious thing is that on being hit, the child screams louder than ever. The distress increases for the child. The child regularly punished for crying, either by a blow or by being rejected, is doubly punished compared to the child who is immediately comforted. In later life such a child will automatically exaggerate any distress or injury.

In truth no one can say if any particular experience in childhood will or will not have damaging consequences later. We do not hear enough of the healthy survivors of awful childhood experiences or really know a great deal about what makes people survive. What we do know is that many people seem to have an extraordinary capacity to adjust, to survive and to heal themselves. The effects of any experience, no matter how damaging it appears—abandonment, sexual abuse, all kinds of cruelty—will always depend on a whole number of factors, essentially on the total context within which the awful event happened. And hope is always affirmed by our constant replaying of experience in the memory or when talking about it.

Early experience can be retrieved and transformed. It can also be used creatively. It is only when we close the discussion by saying, "I'm a failure", "I'm useless", or "I'm a bad person" and no longer question those labels, that our capacity to change is truly diminished. But how a small child learns to deal with her first experiences of distress, how she is responded to when she asks for help in the simple demands of being fed, kept warm, dry and secure, is critical in determining how she will respond to later more difficult encounters with the world.

Take the example of children who are punished for crying when they are hurt. The father or mother who does this is probably intent on producing a brave grown-up. But by punishing their crying child who feels injured, they are liable to produce just the opposite.

The normal response to pain is after all, some kind of cry of distress—ouch! If this is inhibited by fear of disapproval, the fear of the pain itself will increase. Later on in adult life, pain or the possibility of pain will reactivate the memory of more severe distress than would have been the case had the original discomfort and tears been soothed. Men and women being trained to resist torture are taught not to be ashamed or embarrassed about shouting, screaming and displaying the fact that they are suffering. To do that actually increases their resistance to pain.

Women are thought to be more able than men to cope with pain. If that is so, maybe this is because they have, in the past, been allowed to cry out and weep. It is common for women to regard their men as making an inordinate fuss over any injury or illness. It could be that their experience of pain as little boys was linked to the greater pain of humiliation and chastisement.

If a toddler's problem cannot be solved immediately or she is deprived of something she wants, that evokes distress. To have a tantrum, which is a mixture of crying and anger, is a normal response at that stage of development. The toddler is caught between the crying of the helpless infant and the energetic urge for independence of the growing personality.

But some children who have a tantrum may be shaken into terror by an irate adult. So their original frustration becomes connected with fear at being shaken or hit. The adult who has constantly been exposed to this combination may find himself with a weakened ability to tolerate problems and frustration of any kind. The combined burden is too great.

A toddler's tantrums can be coped with. An adult explosion of rage and weeping can be a different matter. The husband whose football team is beaten on Saturday afternoon is distressed. But if he has also invested his identity and status in his team, the threat to his self esteem is intolerable. After drinking heavily he will go home and at the first word of censure, beat up his wife. The same response can occur if a wife is reluctant to share sex. The frustration can ally itself with fear of rejection and violence and rape can result.

So too with encounters between fathers and children. Any situation of disobedience on the part of the child that leaves the father feeling frustrated and helpless may well be dealt with by an explosion of rage, even if the child is only an infant refusing to eat her food.

People who have repeatedly experienced distress and fear being linked together in childhood seem to have particular problems in tolerating the loss of love in adult life. Yet coping with loss is necessary if we are ever to achieve a firm sense of ourselves as individuals who are not utterly dependent on others for approval. The child who has been made to feel fear whenever she feels like crying is especially vulnerable to the threat of separation from the parent who produced the fear/distress link. Some parents spell this out to the crying child—"I'll go away and leave you if you don't stop that noise." Such experiences can lead to extremes of submissiveness in adults, but in adolescence can be the source of outrageous rebellion.

Such people can be made very anxious simply by seeing distress in others. Women describe what happens when they tell husbands that they are not feeling well or are tired—being met with a disgruntled barrage of complaints about his own state of health and fatigue. The wives are seeking sympathy but what they trigger off in their husbands is fear. Those whose own need for comfort as children was not met cannot easily offer comfort to anyone else. One husband with a wife suffering from a progressive paralysis denied her need for care. He refused to change their very heavy manual gear car or move from a totally unsuitable house even when it was obvious she could no longer cope. Another, after an operation for breast cancer, had to conceal from her husband that she was still attending the hospital for follow-up radium therapy. To avoid his anger she would make up her face to look healthy no matter how ill she felt.

Heavy doses of undischarged fear are actually dangerous for the body, but because it is unacceptable for adults to show fear, we erect defences against it. The most common defence is to behave in the opposite way from which we really feel. People who use this defence always appear to be living in the best of all possible worlds, where tiredness, sickness, failure are denied. To maintain this image they will work compulsively or just leave life's rough edges and problems for other people to deal with.

Everything that happens when we link fear and distress can also happen when we link shame with distress. Ordinary human experiences such as sickness, tiredness, solving everyday problems, threats of loss of love, times of loneliness . . . these become doubly difficult to tolerate when shame has been added to distress by the parent who tells us that crying is cowardly, disgusting or babyish. The child who was taught to hang her head in shame because she felt like crying, as an adult is constantly apologising for her existence, heaping contempt on herself when faced with any stressful situation. On the other hand she may defend herself by switching off—claim that there is really never any reason to get upset and just simply avoid taking emotional, physical or social risks. For some people the attraction of mystical religions may be their way of achieving a state of non-involvement with this world. If nothing matters then nothing can cause you distress.

If a child is old enough for the opinion of her carers to matter and her crying meets with a contemptuous response, she will feel a sense of shame. With constant repetition of this contempt a person is created who feels a deep sense of shame. Whenever she has to deal with a difficult situation, she will feel certain that she will fail at anything she attempts. If she finds schoolwork difficult she will feel ashamed. The same reaction will later dominate her work relationships. And just beneath the surface of the shame, tears will be about to burst through.

Some parents, who have the same attitude of shame within themselves, can with the addition of lots of loving attention, use shame as a spur to the child to get their approval and the approval of the rest of the world outside the family. This is effective until the person is confronted by a period of distress that is more than just temporary and before which she feels helpless—a long illness, unemployment , or the death of a child. She is then having to deal with a deep and enduring distress for which she has learned only one response—shame and humiliation.

And if, because of shame, we have suppressed our own tears and unhappiness, we will avoid those of others. If we are forced to notice others' problems, then contempt rather than sympathy is our likely response. The reality of someone else's suffering cannot be borne if one's own has never been accepted. So if not treated with contempt, it will be ignored, side-stepped, the subject of conversation changed. The person complaining, be it friend, partner or child, will be forced to recognise that no comfort will be forthcoming.

Making a child ashamed of tears can sometimes be combined with an emphasis on action to change or improve the situation. The impatient parent or carer may say something like, "Now don't be a cry baby. Crying never solved anything. Stop crying and let's see what can be done. If you stop crying I'll help you." With this kind of approach the child is made ashamed for two reasons. First she is led to feel ashamed just because she is crying. Second, she is ashamed because she is being passive and crying rather than being active and trying to do something about the problem.

Such an approach gives priority to the problem at the expense of the important feelings of pain and discomfort arising from it. People who develop this attitude might well be attracted to law or welfare rights work, areas where practicalities can be dealt with and changed rather than feelings addressed. Someone's problems produce an immediate offer of practical help but no response to their feelings.

There are certain people, well known to Citizens' Advice Bureaux and lawyers, who spend lifetimes in complaint, litigation, and appeals for remedial action. They fill their lives by documenting the wrongs done to them by doctors, dentists, pension boards, social security offices. They exhaust the patience of even the most caring listener but no one, least of all the person himself, is aware that he is constantly on the point of weeping with distress. In his own mind he is perpetually coping with one minor crisis after another, but denies that these have anything to do with the inner life of feeling.

Allowing a child regularly and repeatedly to "cry it out", alone and without comfort, is another way of inducing the shame/distress link that stays with her to some degree for life. If the crying is intense and goes on for a long time until the child ultimately falls asleep or just gives up with exhaustion, the effect is one of apathy and listlessness. What is learnt through the repetition of this experience is that to want something leads to pain and exhaustion.

And there are adults who, when they have difficulty in solving problems, suddenly feel quite tired and exhausted—even to the point of falling asleep. The normal distress that anyone might feel becomes linked to earlier experiences of shame and weariness. This kind of link can also produce a profound resignation to destiny. When you most need help, your experience tells you that your cry for help will not be heard. If it is heard, it will be ignored.

Long continuous experiences of crying to exhaustion will lead to a fundamental pessimism. Such a person is always vulnerable. Someone who has not been allowed to cry in distress will spend much of his life seeking opportunities to cry in ways that do not bring punishment—in sad films, in the tears released when drunk or at funerals. Some of these kind of fantasies might be expressed in sado-masochistic behaviour where in mutual sexual excitement one can hurt and make one's partner cry while being hurt and crying oneself.

The capacity to trust yourself and through that to trust others, is after all the only protection against the ultimate human predicament, our realisation that we are vulnerable and mortal, the awareness that in terms of existence we are alone. Being able to trust, first self, then others, is the basis of all confidence. And it is the basis of all cooperation with and relationships with others. The person who fails to achieve a sufficient level of self-belief is haunted all her life by a sense that she must meet trouble alone, must suffer in silence, can count on no one for sympathy or help. If she were to surrender and cry for help, the fantasy goes, her tears would be met with contempt, hostility or rejection. As an adult this type of person will seek no help from anyone. She will make minimum demands of her doctor, minister or priest and under even the most pressing circumstances will present a "brave" face to the world. If necessary she will even die without complaining.

Some parents take the crying child, comfort it, but make no attempt to find the cause or help the child to understand the problem. The child is given comfort but no solution. If this pattern is repeated, the individual as an adult will continue to look for sedation rather than solutions. When she is lonely, baffled or sick she might find comfort in shopping, eating, alcohol, drugs, body contact with or without sex, warm baths or talking the hours away. Short term comforters can renew energy, but can so easily become addictive alternatives.

chapter seven
Drowning your sorrows

I cry all the time; but deep inside, so no one can see me. I cry all the time. And Georgie cries all the time, too. We both cry all the time, and then, what do we do, we cry, and we take our tears, and we put 'em in the ice box, in the goddam ice trays until they're all frozen and then . . . we put them . . . in our . . . drinks.

Edward Albee

In his powerful and painful play *Who's Afraid of Virginia Wolfe,* Edward Albee describes a marriage in which neither partner can talk about the central pain of their lives. In consequence they communicate with each other through an alcoholic haze which dulls their feelings. But sometimes the pain is so powerful that it breaks through even that protective screen and they are revealed in their naked misery. But we have no sense watching the play that they will be able to grasp the moment and confront the truth of their lives. Instead we realise that they will yet again freeze their tears and plunge themselves with them back into the bottle.

There is an old Eastern story that when the gods created heaven and earth they were left with just one problem—where to hide Truth. They did not want it to be too easy to find since they wanted the fun of watching human beings search for it. One god suggested placing it at the top of the highest mountain; another on the farthest star. A third god said it should be hidden in the deepest and darkest abyss; and another suggested the dark side of the moon. Finally the oldest and wisest god said, "No. We will hide Truth inside the heart of each and every human being. That way they will search for it all over the universe before discovering it."

Another way of telling that story would be to say that people look in all kinds of places to avoid finding the truth and the drug alcohol is one of the easiest to find. The reason for this is that for so many of us the truth of our lives is painful. We want to avoid recognising that fact. The reasons are different for every person. We may feel we are not loved, we may feel our lives are a failure, we may feel we have nothing to live for. For some these feelings comes in middle or old age, for others they come in the earliest years of life.

Laura began to drink at the age of eleven. Her father had walked out of the house after yet another screaming row with her mother and never come back. His loss was a pain which she carried constantly in her breast. She couldn't be angry with him because she could well understand why he had left her mother. She too would have liked to leave her mother. The truth she couldn't face was that he had left her to cope with her mother.

He hadn't loved her enough to protect her and to take her with him.

Her mother's reaction to being abandoned was to move in another man and every night the two of them drank themselves stupid before moving in to the bedroom and having noisy sex. Laura, unable to sleep, would go into the living room and drink anything they had left, the dregs of the whisky bottle and the half empty cans of lager. She found that it helped her to get to sleep. Also she liked the woozy feeling in her head. She didn't mind so much about her father and the pain in her chest disappeared.

By the age of thirteen she was completely addicted. She was not only drinking at night but stealing money from her mother so as to have a can of Carlsberg to drink before she went to school in the morning. She was a very clever girl but her school work deteriorated to the point where her teachers began to ignore her. She used her intelligence to hide her addiction and she began to steal outside the home. By fifteen she was in a children's home, by seventeen she was in a young offender's institution. When she came out she began to work in prostitution as a way of getting money for drink.

Many women working in prostitution drink before starting a shift in order to dull their feelings to the unpleasant nature of the work. But women who have acquired an addiction will not make a successful living since, if they are too drunk, they will not be paid, but raped or their money stolen. This is what happened to Laura and by her early twenties she was sleeping rough and drinking Brasso, sniffing glue, trying anything that would cushion her from the truth of her existence. One winter she was found dead in a building site where she had crawled for shelter.

Laura may seem a rather dramatic example but a recent survey suggests that one third of boys aged 11 have tried drinking when they are unhappy. This is not surprising if we remember that children model their behaviour on what they see adults doing. For adults facing distress the most common reaction seems to be, "God, I need a drink", in the way they used to say, "I need a cup of tea". We see this happening twice a week on the top-ratings BBC soap opera *Eastenders*.

The two main kinds of distress we experience in our lives are physical pain and emotional pain. There was a time when people thought there was no alternative but to live with these as best one could. Religions offered comfort and tried to give distress some sense of meaning. To suffer could bring merit in the after life. But the introduction of anaesthetics and consciousness altering drugs prescribed by doctors changed all that. Suffering seemed unnecessary—there was a pill to deal with any problem. Not only did we become able to avoid physical pain but emotional pain could also be eliminated.

What seems to have been missed is that both types of pain serve a function. Physical pain is essential to diagnose a malfunction of the body. People who can't feel pain have no messages to inform them that they need to attend to their bodies. In the same way emotional pain gives us messages that some part of our inner life needs attention. There are some unfortunate people who never seem able to feel emotional pain. They can behave in inhuman ways as a result.

Once bodily pain is recognised and its cause diagnosed it makes sense to relieve the pain where that is possible. Many aspects of the human body are still mysterious but we know even less about the human mind than we do about the body. It is sensible to be more careful about drugging emotional pain. To cover it up can prevent the real problem being helped. This is what happened to Laura. Her problem was ultimately diagnosed as alcoholism. That was in fact a consequence not a cause. We need to take the emotional life of children much more seriously.

That of course can be difficult when parents do not take their own emotional problems seriously and seek to drown them out with a variety of addictions like work, watching television, food, shopping, sex, gardening, tranquillisers as well as alcohol. But alcohol has a particular power. Why should this be? We need to go back to our earliest experiences to understand it.

Both physical and emotional pain make us question the essential goodness of the world. If we were lucky we found life in infancy safe. By being fed regularly, kept warm and comfortable and comforted quickly when necessary, we learned to trust that this place where we found ourselves was a good place to be. The most regular distress we faced was a feeling of hunger and emptiness. The most important, the most frequent and most comforting experience we had was being fed. We sucked and swallowed streams of liquid which gave us relief from distress and left us feeling blissful. That feeling of bliss stays with us as a distant memory for the rest of our lives.

Distress is usually felt at both physical and emotional levels, neither able to be distinguished from the other. This is always the case for children but even as adults we sometimes find it difficult to distinguish between physical and emotional distress. One of the most common links is between feelings and food. There are people like myself who when unhappy cannot face food. There are others who respond by being ravenously hungry and eating everything in sight to try to lessen the pain.

It is not surprising that there is a link between our feelings and what we take into our mouths. For the first months of our lives our entire survival depends on either the nipple or the teat. Any of us who have watched a small child during its early years knows how everything goes to its mouth. The mouth is full of nerve endings which give all kinds of pleasurable sensations. A child is most easily comforted by having something to suck—its own thumb, a dummy teat, a piece of blanket.

So too with adults. Being fed in restaurants is a great pleasure for most people. Lovers lick and suck each other's flesh. The pleasure of sucking can be so intense that both men and women can achieve orgasm simply by sucking the penis of their partner. Its size in the adult mouth makes it equivalent to the infant experience of the nipple in the mouth. More common sources of pleasure are cigarettes (anyone who has tried to give up knows how strong the sense of oral deprivation can be), pipes, pencils, sweets and any kind of drinks, especially sweet ones.

The sensations created are physical but are also powerful emotionally. We go back to the feeling that the world is a good, safe place. When what we take into our mouths is a substance that quickly affects our brain to relax us and ease us physically the effect is dramatically intensified. The sense of relief is enormous. When it passes and we are left again with the pain, it is natural that we want to get back to that good feeling. Another young woman I knew described to me very vividly how she felt after drinking alcohol. "I just feel so happy," she said. "I feel warm and loved and looked after with nothing to worry about."

Most of Jean's life had not been like that. Her mother had died when she was two years old and she, having no relatives to care for her, was taken into a children's home which had a very strict regime. She was kept clean and fed but they were angry with this bright energetic child when she made a fuss and cried. So she learned not to. Out in the world alone at sixteen, she constantly felt inadequate until her first visit to a pub. With a couple of vodkas inside her she felt able to cope with anything. She became pregnant and managed without drinking while the baby was small and needed her.

The drinking began again when the child started school

and she was alone during the day. Lager would be bought at the supermarket along with the shopping so the child would come home to a mother floating in a private world. In a few years the child was coming home to a mother snoring on the bed. The school teacher began to notice the increasing neglect of the child and notified the social services. The threat of losing the child gave Jean the motivation to begin attending Alcoholics Anonymous and after a hard struggle she's staying off the drink.

Very little attention has been paid to the needs of the children of people who use alcohol to ease their own pain. The emphasis is to find a way of helping the adult. The children, it is assumed, will survive. None of this recognises the terror and despair of the child who sees the person who ought to protect and support them staggering about helplessly. It is worse, in some ways, than being totally abandoned. The body is there but the spirit has gone. This applies also to the children of drug addicts but because alcohol is so much more accepted as a "respectable" drink we take its effects on children less seriously.

What is beginning to be taken seriously is the effects on the foetus of heavy drinking by the pregnant mother. These effects were first noticed in North America where the reservations on which American Indians lived were discovered to have abnormally high levels of brain damaged children. The lives of these women are poor and brutish, desperately deprived. They turn to alcohol to wipe out the horror of day to day existence.

What no one has realised until recently is how damaging

this is to the growing embryo. In this country mothers are now advised to abstain completely throughout their pregnancy.

Total abstention is not easy partly because alcohol is so available. For those of us who want to stay within the law and don't want to go to our doctor to ask for tranquillisers, alcohol is the drug of choice to relieve our pain and misery. At one time of my life I was living in near poverty, in a very bleak place with no friends or relations near to give me comfort when I needed it. Every time I went out to buy food I had to pass a huge street hoarding. All it showed was a hand holding a beautiful crystal glass into which was being poured a golden stream of whisky.

Something happened in my life which left me very depressed and I found myself fixated by this advertisement. Every time I passed it I could imagine how it would feel to taste that golden liquid. I knew how a glow would flow through my veins and most of all I could remember, from past experience, how my head would begin to swim slightly as I drank more deeply. I knew with certainty that my depression would lift.

One day I could resist the temptation no longer. I bought a quarter bottle of whisky which I knew I could not afford. I went home and drank it and for a little while I was released from my misery. The following day I came to my senses and realised how stupid I'd been. But I have never forgotten either the strength of the temptation or the relief I felt as the alcohol entered my blood stream and eased my pain.

One of the great untalked about pains in life is loneliness, particularly the loneliness of those without a partner. Our first experience of life is a pairing with another human being. If we hadn't had that we would have died. This is a model for living that most people carry with them throughout their lives, a model we constantly seek to repeat. We can of course learn to live alone but most people prefer not to.

People are becoming more honest about their need for a partner and will make it known by applying to marriage agencies or by advertising in newspapers or magazines. That is a healthy response. Those who are unable to state their needs openly and perhaps hide them even from themselves may take refuge in numbing their minds with alcohol. This may begin in the simplest way.

Evelyn had been widowed for just over a year. Everyone admired the way in which she had adjusted to her husband's death. She had been very brave, not complaining, going back to work and getting on with her life. Privately it was assumed that she would soon remarry but so far there was no one in sight. She began to have a glass of sherry while watching the news before having supper. She remembered doing this with her husband while he was alive and it seemed to bring him nearer. It did in the sense that it aroused memories which left her feeling sad.

A second glass of sherry seemed to help and it did for a while. Before long the sherry bottle was being half emptied and she didn't bother about supper. She managed to keep a grip on herself during the week but was drinking two bottles of sherry at weekends. It was only when a friend, invited for Sunday lunch, arrived to find her cheerfully staggering about the kitchen, trying to get some food together that she was made to realise that something had gone wrong.

Her friend was a true friend who did not try to pretend that everything was all right. She confronted Evelyn head on and stayed with her until she sobered up. Evelyn wept as she hadn't done even at her husband's death and began to talk with other people about what was happening to her. She still feels lonely sometimes but is now honest about it. She recognises that she may never find another live-in partner but she has moved out to meet people in friendships of a kind she never had when her husband was alive. She has become convinced that, for anyone, drinking alone is dangerous.

I would go further and say that it is not drinking when you're alone that is dangerous but drinking when you feel you're alone in the world even though there are other people there. That was Brenda's experience. She had married when young, convinced she would love Bob for ever. Ten years later there were no children and it seemed there would be none. She worked as a typist in a lawyer's office and began to be aware that there seemed nothing these lawyers were doing that she couldn't do.

One of the partners encouraged her to go to university and take a law degree. She and Bob had some money saved so there were no financial problems. He thought she was daft to bother but didn't try to stop her. What he didn't realise was that it wouldn't be just 9 to 5 but that she would have to study in the evenings. By the second year of her degree he was becoming fed up and saying that this was a mug's game. He began to expect more frequent sex and by ten o'clock was going to bed and shouting to her to hurry up and leave those bloody books alone.

She was consumed with a mixture of anger and guilt which she felt unable to share with him so she began to take a quick swig of vodka before joining him in bed. This numbed her sufficiently to let him penetrate her. She says if she hadn't taken the vodka it would have been impossible. Needless to say her method of anaesthetising herself had to stop if she was to continue studying. It was taking greater and greater amounts of vodka to achieve the same effect as the months passed. Soon she was waking up with headaches and nausea.

She worked up enough courage to go to the university counselling service. She couldn't persuade Bob to come with her for joint counselling. He denied that there was anything wrong with him. It was all her fault—she had become a bad wife. He resolved the problem by moving in with another woman who, he said, didn't have "fancy ideas". Brenda was sad but relieved. She is aware that she escaped a great danger.

Because there is so much alcohol around and we see it in ordinary places like supermarkets and small groceries, we assume it is an ordinary item of consumption like bread or milk or a can of beans. In fact it is a powerful mind altering drug which in earlier societies was used in conjunction with sacred religious services. We use it without respect and live with the fact that alcohol is a central cause of road accidents and deaths, violent assaults on members of the public and private assaults on women and on children.

Used in moderation it eases tension and appears to reduce stress. Conversation flows more easily at a party or round a dinner table. It appears to relax inhibition and ease relationships. The burden of the conscience and of self awareness is lifted. Under its influence we can forget those parts of ourselves we find painful or unattractive. Unfortunately we can also use it as a permanent way of presenting a false self to the world and in the process that other quality of alcohol which is addictive and out of our control can take over. Those people who have overcome an alcoholic addiction have only succeeded in doing so by acknowledging the truth of their own lives no matter how painful that might be and mourning for themselves.

chapter eight
Breaking my heart

Throw out that beggar,
he's breaking my heart.

From the day we are born, we are not only individuals but members of a society that negotiates with us through institutions. The institutions of health, education and housing powerfully influence our lives. Others influence the kind of jobs we get, how much we'll be paid, how we behave in public (and even in private) and how we spend our time and money. Some will even try to influence how we think and feel.

Those who work in institutions, who interface with the public, are usually confronted with people asking for help. This has implications on both sides of the counter, or as is increasingly the case in public offices, both sides of the reinforced glass. On the official side, if we are brought up to think of asking for help as childish and if our requests for help have not been swiftly and cheerfully met, we are less likely to respond in a simple and positive way to demands. If in addition we have been brought up in the tradition that to show feeling is a vulgar and lower class way of behaving, we will seek to drain it out of any situation we are involved in.

The civil service and institutions based on this style see feeling as irrelevant. It is a dangerous complication that must be filtered out. Rules, reason and logic are the principles which are said to govern. But of course such a system ignores the needs of real people who may be full of emotions like fear and helplessness. If ignored, and they generally are, they can turn to public outpourings of tears and anger.

Institutions were set up by people who identify with their aims. And generally they employ staff who are like minded. Even when the staff's own origins and personal outlook are working class, the whole tenor of the service they are operating can be said to lean on a framework which is middle class. When members of the public come in and make demands for services, they will when needs are pressing, express feelings. Certain behaviour like shouting or swearing is regarded by the institution and the officials who work there as "low class" and treated with contempt as "ignorant". Those who manage to present themselves with a cool, unemotional, middle class style have a better chance of their messages being responded to. Some social workers try to teach people codes to use when speaking to a doctor or a magistrate or an official in the housing department.

Some cultures—the Afro-Carribean is one—allow much more open expression of all emotions, laughter, grief and tears. Some working class groups are the same—from the knees-up in the pub to a sing-song on the bus. Appearances on game shows on t.v. are an expression of this working class style—people laugh loudly, show disappointment openly and accept the idea that luck is more important than knowledge. The middle class panel game *Mastermind* demonstrates a rather different view of the world, much more low-key, respectful of specialist knowledge and is really all about respect and status.

Middle class or upper class grief is hidden under controlled facial muscles or even under a black veil. It is as if to let people see your feelings takes away some of your power. By contrast in television pictures of tragedies or at regularly photographed IRA or UDA funerals, working class women are shown weeping with their mouths open, their bodies distorted with grief, part of an ancient tradition. Working class parents whose children are missing, abducted or murdered will appear on t.v. asking for help. They weep openly and harrowingly, unlike middle class parents who are seldom willing to appear, seeing their grief as more private. Each of us lies somewhere on a spectrum of ability to show feeling. And this is often closely related to where we see ourselves on the spectrum of social class.

On the other side of the counter, people who are clearly

powerless and who approach institutions for help, can be treated favourably by the institution if they fit in to expectations and appear subservient. But when the person asking for help is doing so out of desperation or is overwhelmed with anger, a subservient demeanour may be a difficult or indeed objectionable mask to wear.

Some institutions like the Department of Social Security are in a particularly sensitive relationship with the public. Their customers often come to them under considerable stress, dependent, short of money, embarrassed and afraid of rejection. They have waited in an unattractive waiting room for what could be a long time and when they are called to the counter they could be at breaking point. The official may be equally under stress, overworked, resentful, and conscious that the administrative back-up of the office may not be efficient. In such a situation, neither can say what their real feelings are.

So two needy people on either side of a glass screen who are in competition for recognition and support are likely to end up bitter, hostile and dissatisfied. The thought of weeping on each other's shoulders, or at least honestly conceding each other's problems, is not to be tolerated. The applicant goes away complaining vehemently about the unjust and insensitive treatment received. The official retires behind the partition to complain about yet another bad-tempered, ungrateful recipient of state benefits.

Since officials and clerks are not allowed to express their real feelings at work, it's hardly surprising that they can't stand the public screaming in anguish. Any DSS official who sat down and wept with sorrow at the pain they are constantly having to encounter, at the suffering they are daily confronted with, would be considered mentally unstable. The entire structure they are working for depends on the denial of pain—judgement and decisions might be affected. A nineteenth century Rothschild is reported to have said, "Throw out that beggar, he's breaking my heart."

Any sensitive bank manager must have the same feeling. This denial of pain extends to all aspects of life within the workplace. If their own heart is breaking it should not be allowed to show. A parent might be dying of cancer, a love affair might have ended . . . but the pain must not be allowed to leak out.

Some organisations now insist that their staff be constantly cheerful and smiling, no matter how they feel. Staff working the tills in supermarkets are being told that they must smile as they check out each item and as they present the bill. Human beings are expected to be as mechanical as the musak. In one chain of stores, as you make your way out from the staff area into the shop, a notice orders, "Smile! You are now entering the public area."

If staff have good conditions and have an inner motivation to do the job, this could be not an unreasonable request. But it can be a different matter where staff are overworked or underpaid or otherwise feel undervalued. and are still expected to smile constantly. It can come close to what Arthur Haley described in his novel, *Roots.* There the black slaves, no matter how unhappy or angry they felt, as soon as the white man approached began to shuffle and smile so as to look harmless and contented. Not to do so could result in a beating. Will we reach the stage where we see women working supermarket check-outs being sacked because they cannot keep a smile screwed on their faces for eight hours a day?

This insistence on an institutional "brave face" or a "smiling face" presents particular problems for women working in organisations. Women have traditionally been allowed more public expression of feeling than men. But in competing with men for recognition and promotion in the modern organisation they have had to learn to suppress any signs of feminine "weakness". Tears must not be allowed to fill their eyes and under no circumstances run down their cheeks. The male mafia will close ranks and deem such a woman unstable, neurotic and quite unsuitable for responsibility. Even if she has a male boss who has tantrums, a boss who shouts and bullies her, in the institutional world of male values she will lose all respect if she cries. She may know that her tears will relieve her tension more effectively than shouting back or pretending not to notice. No matter. Nor will it matter if her tears are tears of anger rather than vulnerability. Nor will concession be made to pre-menstrual weepiness. To draw attention to that would only compound the woman's error.

The problem for women is highlighted by the case of a thirty year old trainee RSPCA inspector, dismissed because she wept when dogs were put to death. She appealed against her sacking under the Sex Discrimination Act but lost her case. Mary Warnock the philosopher argued that the dismissal was justified since professionals must learn to face a work demand like mercy-killing with calm. She thought it very bad for the image of women that they should always be seen as the people most likely to follow their hearts and not their heads. Women she argued, should practise not crying except in exceptionally worthy circumstances.

Yet those tears which led to the inspector's dismissal could have been seen as a source of energy and redirected by an understanding supervisor to a powerful commitment to doing the work well. I would certainly rather have an RSPCA worker who retained the capacity to weep than one hardened to the darker necessities of the job.

Geraldine Bedell, writing in *The Independent* newspaper, described what happened when the senior partner of a law firm was confronted with tears from an exhausted female colleague at the conclusion of a marathon deal. "How can I ever treat her quite the same again?" he said. "There's always this fear she won't be able to cope, so you don't give her the difficult jobs."

She describes another incident where a woman, reduced to tears by a senior colleague, began to realise that he was enjoying seeing her cry. Bedell writes that when a man embarks on one of those humiliation rituals that men behind desks have been perfecting for generations, she wishes she had the guts to introduce a bit of power play and weep gently but composedly. Why, she asks, give up this healthy show of emotion for heart attacks?

But many men in the workplace are genuinely afraid of tears. Some are afraid of their own tears and the abyss that would open if they once made contact with their own pain. For others, seeing a woman cry revives hidden feelings about seeing their mothers cry. Such memories cover very complicated feelings of helplessness, the awfulness of seeing the most important person you depend on in acute distress. A Colin White cartoon shows a woman weeping copiously over a man at a desk who is hiding under an umbrella and waving a white flag.

There may be feelings of anger aroused in some men when they see a woman cry. In his book on Robert Maxwell, Joe Haines describes how Maxwell's normally imperturbable secretary burst into tears after a spell of work when he had been even more demanding than usual. Maxwell walked into her office and found her crying. "Who's done that to you? he demanded angrily. "I'll sack him."

As women return to work in institutions after having their own children, they perform extraordinary emotional gymnastics. In their daily lives with children they engage freely and fully in basic feelings of love, anger, frustration, fury, pain and joy, often coupled with tears. They learn to do several things at once. They use skills with their children of conciliation, negotiation, and contract. They recognise the usual pointlessness of confrontation with a small person who doesn't understand the assumptions the adult is operating on. They develop a capacity to respect passing joys and they respect happy chance happenings. They know how helpful tears are to defuse tension and how constructive their aftermath can be. The healing quality of tears and laughter is part of their lives.

None of these skills tend to be recognised by their male colleagues in the workplace. So women often abandon them as they try to fit into organisational patterns that make no sense to them but which they are constantly assured are superior. Sometimes women use what they have learned to "handle" male colleagues but few are able to influence the masculine value base of their workplace. So since women are often happier working together and they reject the driven competitive style that sacrifices family and fun, they are reluctant to fight their way into senior management positions.

Of course, we are learning that the way institutions are organised is increasingly a problem for men as well as women. Institutions that concede no place for feelings and assume that private and public have to be kept separate, are not healthy for anyone. In fact failure to address emotional issues will get in the way of achieving the organisation's goals.

The British Empire was built on the unshed tears of small boys in preparatory and boarding schools. It was a terrible price to pay but most defend the legacy of ideas of fairness, justice and good government they took to others round the world.

chapter nine

Gender traps

What in the world is the use of a creature
All flabbily bent on avoiding the pitch
Who wanders about with a sob in each feature
Devising a headache, inventing a stitch?
There surely would be an end to my joy
If possessed of that monster—a feminine boy.

Norman Gale

The Female Boy from *More Cricket Songs* (1905)

Woman after woman has told me how their partners can't bear to see them cry. "If I cry, he just walks out," says one. "If I cry, he gets so angry that I can't bear it," says another, "and I go away and find somewhere by myself where I can go on crying."

"But it's a terrible feeling," says another, "not to be able to cry with the most important person in your life. The tears aren't the same somehow if you've got to cry alone. They don't heal you in the same way if you can't share them."

These women saw their tears as an important release from tension, yet they had been unable to persuade husbands or partners to be comfortable when they were crying, just to be there and let them cry. "He always wants to do something to stop me crying," is a frequent comment. "If I'm crying because someone's been nasty to me, he'll want to rush away and knock their block off," said one woman. "For anything else, he'll just sit there and look miserable and uncomfortable until I feel I'm supposed to comfort him!"

It becomes clear talking with women that many men find it difficult to offer comfort. They seem unskilled in the simple acts that console women when they are distressed—like being held gently for as long as they need to be held, just giving comfort. From what women say, the help that is most useful is non-verbal. Sounds are all right but words, especially logical words in sentences, tend to be of not much use in the initial stages of crying. It seems that the important thing is an unhurried, quiet, non-judgemental and shared experience.

Most women offer this to each other when they cry together. To watch women comfort each other can be a deeply moving experience. Understanding of each other's needs may be related to earlier good experiences of being comforted by their own mothers. But presumably men were comforted in the same way. So why are they, unlike women, unable to pass it on?

For some men, the tears of women with whom they are

closely involved may arouse anxiety, provoking memories of their mother crying. This may reactivate feelings of helplessness and fear because the person to whom they look for comfort is herself vulnerable. Some unhappy women, whose husbands are unable to offer them emotional support, quite inappropriately turn to their sons. The conflict aroused in these boys can bring on an emotional paralysis in later life.

And equally, the buried temptation invoked by the seductive mother may result in the same man being profoundly moved and sexually attracted to distressed women for whom he has no emotional responsibility. Few things are more infuriating for a woman who is denied comfort for her own tears than to see her partner being sympathetically and sensually attracted to a strange woman who is grieving—widows, divorcees, or unhappily married women. What the sorrowing woman who is the object of this attention has to realise is that if the grieving or suffering stops, or if intimacy develops to the point of involving responsibility, such men's interest often evaporates.

It may be that the defences against their own feelings makes it impossible for men to tolerate the intense show of feeling from their weeping women partners. If you are not allowed that kind of release for yourself, it may be intolerable to see someone else doing it.

Men are taught from their earliest days to value autonomy, the right to do what they want to do, when they want to do it. Women, because of the nurturing and caring roles allocated to them, are much more likely to be taught the value of submitting to one's fate and considering the needs of others before their own. That states the gender positions very crudely. In fact, both are extremely complex. They are described in many other ways—as yang and yin, as materialism and spirituality, as individualism and cooperation. They can be blended creatively, but too often they are poorly understood styles of behaviour acted out between men and women as conflicting opposites. Tears from the woman, which with more understanding can create a bridge between the two positions, more often intensify the barriers.

Certainly the route to manhood is hard for small boys. Like girls they start life locked into the warm sensual bliss of their mother's body, emotional and responsive. But by two years of age they have learned that they don't belong in that world. They learn to be not like their mothers, warm and receptive; they have to be like their father whose body is hard, not soft, who is energetic, not passive, and who is powerful, not weak. Later in life the theory goes, he will be allowed to go back to the softness of a woman's body. But by then he will be strong and be able to dominate her. If the conditioning has been successful, he will be able to take what he wants, not plead for it like a baby. If he fails to learn how to dominate a woman, he will have failed to realise the most powerful myth of masculinity. Most families tell small boys quite clearly what is expected of them . . . autonomy and aggression. Girls are expected to be docile and sweet, hiding their aggression and anger because it's not tolerated.

One observer points out that if you took a baby out into

the street and stopped the first twenty people and asked them to hold "Mark", and then ask them to tell you what sort of baby he is, they would describe him as bouncing, cheeky, mischievous and strong. Do the same thing with the same baby but call it "Mary" and the responses will be that she is lovely, sweet, gorgeous, cute.

Later nurseries and schools reinforce gender roles. Teachers and other adults begin to withdraw warmth and open affection from the small boys as a way of encouraging "manly" behaviour. Although at this early age, biological factors are not thought to cause differences, boys behave in much more aggressive ways than the girls. Boys also seem to learn early that it is better, more interesting, if you're a boy rather than a girl. This means that qualities associated with girls—passivity, gentleness, caring, the show of affection and feeling—are seen as inferior ways of behaving and must be avoided. After they start school, mothers are seldom allowed to kiss boys in public.

When, as inevitably happens with younger boys in school, some failure or humiliation invokes tears in the classroom, the other boys freeze with embarrassment. But later in the playground they may persecute the weeper remorselessly. He has acted out their worst fears for themselves.

Young males develop the need to protect themselves from thoughts or information that might trigger off feeling vulnerable. Many boys find it difficult to listen to each other. Almost before a sentence is finished they are challenging, deriding, contradicting. Listeners to

Parliamentary broadcasts will recognise the phenomenon.

The emotional life of men is a neglected area of study. Everyone takes it for granted that men don't cry as much as women but few question why that should be. Yet just as women can become trapped into roles of passivity and being dependent, so men are trapped into responsibility and strength. In times of severe hardship or danger, it is as if men's tears can't be tolerated lest they weaken determination to fight and struggle—as if to fight and struggle with full force demands that all tender feelings have to be abandoned. In our culture, manliness has become linked with control of feelings, courage, assertion and being able to endure without complaint. Darwin, who viewed tears as being rather lowly on the evolutionary scale, placed the Englishman at the peak of progress because he only wept "under the pressure of the most poignant moral suffering", whereas, "in certain parts of the Continent men would shed tears with great ease and abundance."

I asked a number of men living in Scotland about their tears. They had been meeting regularly to discuss their conflicts about masculinity. Few could remember very early experiences of crying. Where they did it centred on being left alone either by their mothers or whoever was caring for them. For some, their earliest memories were of being beaten by their father and shouted at for crying while the beating was going on.

One man's story was particularly poignant. His first memories of tears were to do with being savagely beaten whenever his father returned home from a sea voyage.

After her death he realised his mother had not bequeathed him a single act of kindness. She would present his father with a catalogue of the sins and misdemeanours the child had committed since his last visit home. His task on the first day of his return was to take the small boy to an unused bedroom and without saying a word, unbuckle his leather belt and ritually beat him with it. After years of silence, this man now weeps readily, but only for situations bound up with injustice.

Many of the men I talked with had been derided as children for crying and spent years swallowing or hiding their tears. One, now a successful businessman, was one of the many victims of British imperialism. The only child of a civil servant stationed in the Far East, he was left at the age of four in a children's home in this country. He remembered his mother leaving in a red car and then not seeing her for months. She did not say goodbye as "that would only have encouraged emotion". He trained himself not to cry and not to feel. By the age of six he finally managed to prove himself capable of resisting pain. Brought by his parents to a school in the Far East, he would allow the other boys to fire arrows made out of thorns into his bare legs. He would stand there in his short trousers and not make a sound. Looking down at the arrows sticking in his legs he knew that he had successfully vanquished feeling. He had made himself impenetrable and the other boys had admired him for it. His distance from his own feelings lasted for forty-four years, when at last he was able to cry as he told the story.

There are of course many men who are able to offer

comfort and who are at ease with their partner's tears. We know little about them, presumably because their partners do not complain. It is fair to speculate a little about what kind of men these may be. They are probably at ease not only with women's tears but with a range of private feelings and needs. They probably have enough inner strength not to feel threatened by the demand for child-like dependency implicit in tears—they will recognise it for what it is, a temporary need rather than a permanent threat to their autonomy. They will not automatically feel manipulated. Most importantly, the event will be experienced by them as a reality that is happening in the here and now and not as a replay of frightening and damaging early experiences. The will see the actual woman who is crying as herself and not as some emotional ghost from the past. They will probably be able to respect their own tears and if they have children will be able to respect theirs. One young woman who talks lovingly about her tears told me how her father used to say, "It's Fred inside you watering the iris in his window boxes."

Yet one of the hardest things for women to bear is the way men reject tears as silly and irrelevant, when they know them to be important and valuable. "Why do I cry?" answered one woman. "I cry to release huge waves of feelings that can build up, especially when I cannot or dare not put feelings into words. The dare-not feelings are usually anger. I fear it will go out of control so I release it in tears by myself or with someone I love and trust. If I'm angry with someone I love and trust, I can express my anger in tears with them. If I'm angry with someone I do not love, then I withhold my tears—to be expressed later in a safe situation, or not at all. If I hold back the tears, the feeling becomes locked or blocked in my body."

Another adds to the story— "I can't stress too much the value I give my tears . . . they are priceless beyond words. They are the most private part of myself that I can share with those who draw close to me. They give me life and hope, they renew me."

These are women holding onto the value of tears. But there are many others who have been made to feel ashamed. The most frequent messages given to women are that tears are a sign of weakness, or instruments of manipulation. One young woman who uses tears very creatively in her life and also in her work as an actress asserted very positively, "I don't think that crying is a sign of weakness as it's so often made out to be. It's a sweet strength like my body's poetry. It's at the edge of things."

Tears are clearly woven through her life in a natural way. "Sometimes," she explained, "I go without crying for some while and then I go through phases of crying a lot. Of course tiredness affects it as do my periods and the time of day even. Sometimes my tears are so hot they feel as if they've been baking inside me, sometimes they feel bigger and wetter, sometimes rather lighter and not so salty. Sometimes I have to make a lot of noise with them and move my body with them like passion—and sometimes they just slide out very gently and don't affect me so much, like a cooling system."

In this extraordinarily intuitive and perceptive account of her relationship with her tears this young woman has confirmed many of the research findings of scientists interested in the physiology of tears. She sees her tears as meeting a variety of her needs. She recognises how they interact with her body chemistry, tiredness or her period. Different kinds of need alter the quality and the quantity of the flow. She uses her tears as a natural antidote to tension and stress which is one of their most important functions.

Women who get relief and even enjoyment from crying can share this given only modest encouragement. One day when I had first begun to question people's tears, the assistant in a Glasgow clothes shop, an attractive and helpful young woman, asked what kind of work I did. I explained that I was writing a book about the part tears play in our lives. Her face lit up.

"Oh, I love my tears," she said. "I cry all the time, when I'm happy, when I'm sad, when I'm making love. It's terribly important to me." She told me of the one time when the weeping stopped. When she was about twenty, she worked in an office, one of two women among about thirty men. Late one afternoon, after a particularly demanding day, she sat down at her desk and burst into tears. The other woman, whom she described as a man-hater, made her get up and come to the lavatories and once inside shouted vehemently, "Don't you ever do that again. If those men see you crying they'll walk all over you." The shock was such that she stopped crying immediately. But what was worse was that she stopped crying at home as well and felt simply awful, physically and mentally, until able to cry again.

I asked her if her husband minded her tears. "He's used to it now," she said. "At first he was frightened. Especially when I wept after we'd made love. He'd ask if he'd hurt me, but now he's used to me." And she laughed with pleasure.

chapter ten
Love and loss

(Wo)man is not destroyed by suffering. (S)he is destroyed by suffering without meaning.

What Albert Camus might have said

"Robert didn't say I must go back to work after the baby," Lucy told me, "but he began to be reluctant about switching on electric fires and looking disapproving if I did. He took over total control of the finances and the cheque book. I had to account for every penny I spent, but he never told me what he was spending. He started leaving a ten pound note on the table every morning when he went out to work. Some mornings he would rush away and forget to leave anything. If I noticed in time I would have to run after him and ask for it. I would come back into the house feeling so humiliated that I would just sit down and cry and then the baby would start crying so I would have to stop.

"For the first time in our marriage I began to tell him lies. I had a little money saved and I began to use it up. When I bought something I'd say it was less than it really was. I wouldn't tell him if I went for lunch with my mother or a girl friend and I paid. I couldn't bear that they should always pay for me because I didn't want them to know how awful Robert had become. Then my money ran out and I stopped going out at all. I got more and more depressed. Sex was awful. If I didn't want it he would say that he was keeping me and the least I could do was give him sex. So after that I just lay there and let him do what he wanted and he would complain about that too. He would go to sleep and I would lie there with tears running down my face thinking how good it had been before the baby came. If I tried to talk to him, I used to start crying and he would say, "Oh God!" and tell me I was useless."

With the help of a friend Lucy stopped crying and started being angry. She found a childminder and went back to work. She doesn't cry in front of Robert any more. She still tells him lies about what things cost so that she can save money and make sure she'll never be dependent on him again. She has also decided not to have a second baby.

Lying in bed after sex, silently weeping when your partner has gone off to sleep is an experience many women are familiar with. The sexual life of the young exhausted mother of a fractious baby takes on a dream-like quality.

"I'm too tired even to object," said one drained looking young woman, "He just keeps telling me that he loves me and needs me. All I can think of is not wakening the baby, so I say OK and he goes ahead. One night I was so tired that I fell asleep when he was still pushing in and out of me. I wakened up when he started shouting. Then he turned away and went to sleep and I lay there and wept, feeling an absolute failure."

Women recognise that some of their tears are tears of weakness. These are the tears that come as an alternative to rage and anger or as a way of coping with their feelings of powerlessness. Most women find it very difficult to express anger openly and honestly, especially to men. They also find it hard to cope with men who are angry with them. Women learn at an early age that most men do not like angry women living in the same house. In abstract they may admire and be excited by them, but their day-to-day preference is for women who want to please them and don't make too much fuss. Modern men also stipulate that they mustn't be boring without seeing any contradiction.

Girl children learn these messages in subtle ways. The most obvious is by watching father's reaction to mother's behaviour and the comments of both about other women and other marriages. But the most powerful message is father's reaction to his daughter's femininity and the part she may have to play as "daddy's little girl". Often the more charming, cuddly, loving and even manipulative she is, the more rewarded. "She can twist me round her little finger," is said with glowing pride. Very few fathers would actually prefer to have a strong-minded, independent daughter who put her own needs before his and was able to criticise his behaviour openly.

So girls learn not to show anger and repress it. The women who talked to me about using their tears to deal with anger, recognised quite clearly what they were doing. Most either thought it didn't matter as long as they got relief for their tension and frustration and saw it as a way of keeping the peace. But some were trying to express themselves more honestly. They had become aware of their fear of sharing feelings with their partners and saw this as an unhealthy way to live

For women there are few ways of improving the balance of power within the family (or within the workplace). For those unable to be direct, the bed can become, for the angry woman, an arena of struggle, perhaps the only one in which she has the advantage. She can if she chooses convert the pain, the humiliations, the tears of every other situation in which she is disadvantaged, into revenge, contempt and victory. Unless the partner is a violent man, the woman can dictate how often sex will take place. The cynicism that grows out of not having tender feelings acknowledged and valued replaces the openness and tenderness with which she first entered into the partnership.

"Twice a month's about right for me. That satisfies my sexual need which is actually stronger than some of my friends, and it's often enough to take the edge off him. What I don't want is to do it so seldom that he gets angry. Because he does if he has to wait too long. Also I don't want him to have it off with someone else. I've cried enough trying to get him to understand that there's a difference between a good fuck and a good shit."

Most partnerships involve tentative negotiations until they find ways of communicating what suit each other's needs. Mostly these are the best that can be managed. Tears become a signal to the male partner that the issue under discussion is one that should be taken seriously, and if he is sensitive to his partner's needs he will respond swiftly and allow the woman to weep in ways that affirm her dignity. One husband described to me how he has learned to interpret the various kinds of tears his wife sheds.

"When she's crying with pain for something like a migraine headache, I just sit in the dark with her and hold her hand. If she's been crying for some other reason like because we've been quarrelling and she wants to make up but doesn't know how to, I just put my arms round her and cuddle her and let her cry it out. Until she's done that I know I won't get any sense out of her. I try to work out if she's got a period due or if she's been having trouble with her mother. If we've been quarrelling, after she's stopped crying I really try to understand what she was on about. It must mean a lot to her if it made her cry."

That's a very different response from thc man whose anxiety or guilt are aroused by his partner's tears and shouts, walks away, or who gives in to the woman's demand without trying to understand what's "going on". Handling things in this way is likely to leave him with a sense of confusion and resentment. She in turn may hope that in time she will get the caring response she is really seeking and will pursue the pattern. Such a tragic game can go on for years unless one decides that enough is enough and withdraws.

Time and again discussions about tears came back to the central theme of the wish to be cared for—not all the time, the women I talked with were quite clear about that. But what they all wanted was to be cared for some of the time and often their tears were statements about that need. It seemed rather a simple and healthy statement of a basic need in a relationship to be nourished by one's partner.

Feminists argue that women should not be so dependent on the opinion of men. A woman's sense of validity should lie in her feelings about herself. While this may be true, we should remember the fragility of the human psyche. Even if someone becomes self-confident and inner-directed, that has to be constantly reinforced if those attitudes are to be maintained. A year at home with a small child and no recognition by a partner of the importance and difficulty of that role can reduce the most competent career woman to an anxious or depressed wreck.

Shortcomings in recognising feelings are of course not only a problem between men and women, and such things are not confined to personal relationships. The world of work, if the job involves powerlessness on one side, throws up the same patterns. But it is true to say that for most women, the most powerful source of their tears lies in their relationship with men. And especially so in experiences of feeling abandoned.

To lose love through death is hard but understandable. To lose love and not understand why is intolerable. For many it is a situation that induces a kind of frenzy. The abandoned lover may weep until she can weep no more. She may rage, scream, become ill. What is wanted more than anything else is to understand why this has happened. And some will go to extraordinary lengths to try to find out.

If a woman's relationship with a man breaks down and he abandons her, she will usually blame herself, having been taught that success in personal relationships is her responsibility. If she has lost her partner to another woman, it will be assumed that she must be more beautiful, more clever, more sexy. In fact she wants her to be. That would make sense.

A stunning young woman whose husband left her for a woman twenty years older than himself, never forgave him for it. He had questioned a fundamental tenet of her life, that young women are more attractive than older women. Her self-confidence never recovered, since if her belief was right there must have been something else wrong with her, some terrible ugliness from which he had fled even into the arms of an older woman.

Where the other woman is not known, fantasy can run riot. The other becomes a witch, an evil enchantress, with amazing powers to seduce the innocent. Efforts are made to find out more about her, sometimes with extraordinary ingenuity. The energy put into this can be manic in quality, a white heat of power that other women will understand but most men will find frightening.

Ann's lover simply stopped coming to see her, giving her no explanation. The relationship on his side had clearly been casual, never serious or even regular, but she became very emotionally involved and hoped it would develop. She tried phoning him with a variety of invitations she felt he wouldn't refuse, but he always made excuses for not meeting her. Knowing something of his work and leisure habits, she tried meeting him "accidentally" coming out of his workplace or at his local pub, all to no avail.

She became convinced that he had found another woman and concentrated on trying to find out who she was. She sent him theatre tickets for two anonymously and bought herself one for a few seats further back. Two strangers used the seats. She took to following him in her car, being willing to sit for hours outside his house waiting for him to come out and then trailing and following him until he came home again. All her energy was focussed on his life and what he was doing. Her own life and work faded into insignificance. One night, waiting in her car outside the pub where she'd followed him, she suddenly found herself crying for the first time. She says she wept non-stop for an hour during which she gradually came to realise she had been out of her mind for the last six weeks. As she wept she allowed the pain of the loss of her man to become real. She went home and the next morning began rebuilding her life.

Jane had been sharing her life and home with a partner John, for four years. His firm sent him for a month to another part of the country and at first he telephoned home every night. But after three weeks she got a letter saying that he had met another woman and was planning to marry her as soon as possible. She can't remember how she spent that day but has a vague memory of being like a wild animal howling through the house, tears pouring down her face, drinking brandy, tearing at her clothes, pulling his clothes out of the wardrobe and holding them close to her, burying her face in them, trying to recover the smell of him. The prophet Micah's image of desolation is very similar—"Therefore I will wail and howl, I will go stripped and naked. I will make a wailing like the dragons, and mourning as the owls." Terrified to phone him and hear him say the words he had written on paper, she collapsed ultimately into a drunken stupor—a woman who had never before drunk more than half a bottle of wine.

For several days she stayed off work and continued to weep helplessly until exhausted. Her head gradually began to clear. She resolved to find out about the other woman. She had almost lost interest in the man but felt obsessed with the woman who had made such an impression in such a short time. Her partner's hobby was shooting, and she knew from their phone calls that he had been spending his spare time at a sports club which had a range. Her brain was more active than ever before. She hunted down the phone number through directory enquiries and then rang. She asked for the secretary and launched on a long story about phoning from a restaurant where a pair of leather gloves had been left apparently by the lady with Mr Johnston whom one of the waiters had remembered seeing at the sports club. Would the secretary know if Mr Johnston had a wife who might have been with him?

The secretary laughed and said he thought he could guess who that was. No it wasn't Mr Johnston's wife. He didn't have one. His guess was that they belonged to another of their members. Should he pass a message on? "No," said Jane, "but if you could give me her number I'll ring and arrange to have them returned."

"No trouble," was the response and the number was found. Jane could hardly believe it had been so easy. The next step was to phone. When a woman's voice answered, she had to hang up, her anger was so powerful. She sat down to recover but it was an hour before she could dial again.

This time she was prepared and she launched quickly into a story that she was a freelance journalist doing an article for the women's page of a national newspaper about women who joined sports clubs. Could she do a telephone interview? It worked and for the next half hour she was able to quiz the woman whom she saw as having stolen her happiness on every aspect of her life. What distressed her most was that she began to find herself liking the woman. She realised they had much in common. She continued to weep and suffer for many months but the tears were no longer helpless but purposeful. Her first insane reaction to the loss had eased when she confronted the reality of the other woman and the new tears played an essential part in her healing.

These women and many others behaved in ways that are completely out of character. They sent anonymous letters, daydreamed about how to damage or poison the other person or find some way of ruining their lives. What is extraordinary is how seldom the anger is unleashed on the partner, the one responsible for the loss. Sometimes women turn their anger against themselves as in the pain of bereavement, take overdoses of sleeping pills, cut their hair short, rake their skin with their fingernails, feeling that physical pain is more tolerable than emotional pain. The tension is most frequently released in tears.

Another woman, whose lover went back to his wife wept herself to sleep every night for six months. Every morning, exhausted but able to cope, she struggled to work. Bitterly ashamed of her failure to hold his love, she couldn't bring herself to discuss what had happened with even her closest friends. She used her weeping time before sleep for long conversations inside her head in which she began to make sense of what had happened.

If we are lucky we have someone in our lives with whom we can shed healing tears. Women are fortunate. They can usually find another woman to share the pain. Men are less so. They not only have to cope with the cultural fear showing emotion, but also with dismissive and often lewd attitudes to women that surround them. They may find someone they can talk to, but rarely someone with whom they can cry.

This is why men who have been deeply hurt in an extra marital affair often have a compulsion when it ends to tell all to their wives in a great burst of weeping. The purpose is less to get forgiveness than to get some relief from the tension and the pain. They turn to the one person who may accept their tears without judgement. Some, who may be kinder, will find a way of weeping in their wives' arms without explaining the cause. The wife may have a shrewd idea, but might just offer comfort without choosing to seek out the source of the pain.

Shame is at the heart of much of the grieving done by women when men leave them. Its core is in the sense of rejection of the most private and intimate part of themselves, because that is what women in love offer so generously to men. "I gave him everything I had but it wasn't enough," is the grieving statement of the jilted woman.

Men in love may offer a great deal but they seldom make such a full commitment. They are much more likely to hold on to a degree of independence. They'll cite the importance of their work, their politics, their hobbies and interests, their nights out with "the boys". They seldom give to the relationship the commanding priority that women feel, particularly in the early stages of loving. The intensity of love that some women feel puzzles many men. Flattered for a little while, they soon begin to feel embarrassed or threatened by the powerful force that surrounds them. It seems to arouse expectations that they feel they can't meet. It makes demands on them. They want life to be simpler.

For the women on the other hand, this kind of love, if only it could be returned, opens up possibilities of finding a kind of heaven on earth, a healing of past wounds, a gateway into full intimacy with one other person, an end to existential dread and isolation.

chapter eleven
Corridors of power

. . . unashamedly, loudly, wetly - as spasm after spasm of misery washed over me. What would happen to me? What would become of me? What had I done? Why didn't it stop? Nobody seemed to be in control . . . All these big, strong, wise doctors were supposed to be in charge, they were supposed to be helping me—that was the only compensation for the humiliating procedure I'd had to endure.

Hospitals, with some marvellous exceptions among their staff, have clung by and large to old patterns of training where the doctor protects himself from the patients' feelings of discomfort, loss and terror in the face of illness and death. Medical students who show their own distress and pain at the plight of the patient are identified as unsuitable or unprofessional and are expected to "harden up". Many learn to protect themselves from patients' questions by always being very busy or emotionally unapproachable. Patients, particularly women who are conditioned from childhood to be accepting rather than questioning, are given the sense that they musn't try to invade medical territory.

As long as doctors hold onto the role of being omnipotent, it's not surprising they need defences. It is a great burden for them if they cannot share their uncertainty about a complicated diagnosis, or their distress if they have to predict an inevitable death or permanent disability. An oncologist may have to diagnose a malignant tumour several times a day. An opthalmologist may have to tell five patients, in one morning clinic, that they are going blind. In any outpatient department on any day of the week, people are being given life-or-death judgements about their future.

The attitude of the doctors usually forces patients to conceal their feelings like those of the woman at the head of this chapter. Any whose feelings overflow are liable to be seen as "weak" or "difficult". "Courage" is the cliche for the response of silent grief and suffering that is admired. It makes life easier for everyone.

I asked an eye specialist, a thoughtful and genuinely caring man, how patients responded to going blind. Do they cry, I asked him.

"They probably do," he said, "but I can't let them cry with me when I've got a queue of people." I tried to find out if there was any place in the hospital where they could have gone to weep and share their distress. In fact, although many hospitals have chapels, there was no such refuge that he was aware of. It may have been that people went to the lavatory to cry, or left it till on the bus back home.

The most common defence against feeling for hospital doctors is to see the symptom but not the patient. A friend of mine, admitted for investigation of a lump on her breast, refused to give automatic permission for a masectomy. On his next round of the ward, the surgeon said bluffly, "What's all this about? After all, at your age you're not going to need your breast any more!" My friend was then a very attractive, unmarried woman of forty-one. Controlling her anger, she looked at him and said, "You're older than me. Do you want to keep your testicles?"

He swept away and she never saw him again in the hospital. Six months later, having kept her breast intact, she was at a party when the surgeon appeared on the other side of the room. She made her way over to him. He had no recollection of her and began to flirt mildly. Not being a woman to miss an opportunity, she described their previous meeting. He didn't appreciate the joke and left the party early.

Not all women are as strong-minded as my friend. Stories brought back from gynaecological examinations confirm that expressions of pain during examination rouse irritation or accusations of neurosis. One woman writing to a women's magazine told of her distress at a particularly dehumanising experience. The female nurse was aware of her humiliation and kept throwing sympathetic glances. She finished her letter by saying that this must seem a very small matter to people suffering from serious illnesses but she resented not feeling able to complain because of her fear of being seen as childish or neurotic. As happens with children, her fear was compounded by being made to feel ashamed.

The greatest problem, especially for surgeons, is the patient who has not been helped by an operation and is now dying. There seems to be no place for a dying person on the surgical wards. It is almost as if, having failed, the staff cannot bear to see the patient. It is too great a challenge to their image of themselves as healers. They are trained only to cure, to treat and prolong life. They are taught nothing about helping people to die. Their response is sometimes brutal.

It was made clear to a friend of mine who was dying that he was not wanted on the ward—not through words, but by being given minimum care after an unsuccessful operation and the refusal of any doctor to speak to him. He knew that staff were avoiding him. His wife was asked, by a junior consultant who could give no information about the operation, to take him home. She is herself a nurse, not by any means inarticulate, but she could get no one to speak or to tell her anything. She described it as a nightmare. Ultimately her GP intervened and she was told that the outlook was hopeless. He persuaded her to take her husband home where he died within a few weeks.

One of the most distressing factors is the "jollying up" attitude of medical and nursing staff. It is a commonplace experience of hospitals that patients and their families will collude with the ritual pretence that everything is for the best in the best of all possible worlds.

A pregnant woman whose baby had died in the womb was not told that her baby was dead until after it was born. The staff thought it better to let her go through her labour cheerfully. One nurse described how she always knocks at the door of a private room if there is a terminally ill patient—in case she should catch them crying. "I don't want to embarrass them," she said.

Beata Bishop, in her book *A Time to Heal,* writes about her experience of cancer. Before she was ultimately cured using alternative healing methods, she tells of her experience of conventional surgery. After her operation the surgeon called in to see her every day. She describes it thus:

Looking back, I find it interesting that our exchanges were consistently humorous, as if we had been rehearsing for a Wit and Wisdom contest. I was acting out the role of the good courageous patient as I saw it at the time, while Mr Lennox was no doubt pleased to find me co-operative, free from despair and, above all, unemotional. I played this game and he rewarded me with encouraging remarks about my cancer-free future.

Even while this game was being played out, Beata Bishop knew intuitively that she was not cured. The cancer re-emerged in her groin within a year. She found within herself a healing power that she allied with alternative therapies and is now fully cured.

These kinds of experiences are familiar to anyone who

has ever had anything to do with institutionalised medicine. Roles of knowing, expert professional on the one hand and submissive, helpless and compliant patient on the other are enacted by the main characters concerned. The examples are based on hospital experiences but will be recognisable to and applicable to other institutions where human beings are looked after or meet to achieve some mutually agreed task. Schools, centres for the pre-fives, work organisations, residential care homes, prisons, churches and religious organisations—all human institutions betray to some degree or other, the attributes that have been described for hospitals.

None of this behaviour adopted by professionals is intended to be unhelpful. The rationalisation is that everything is done in the interests of all, but the various expectations, rules and procedures are also designed to protect professionals from feelings that are, for them, genuinely intolerable. In hospitals the rationalisation is that this helps patients. The reality is that it doesn't. What the patients need is to have emotional fear and pain acknowledged and expressed through words, tears or in whatever other way they find helpful.

Stephanie Cook in her book *Second Life* describes after a harrowing time in hospital an encounter with a nurse who didn't need such high defences.

What a relief to be able to complain . . . openly, freely, to say how I really feel! [She] . . . will not interpret my sharing of my pain as an assault, she will not turn away or urge me to be strong, or murmur some expression of sympathy or swallow hard because there is, finally, nothing to say to someone who is beyond comfort thought not beyond caring.

One way of avoiding anxiety is not to acknowledge individuals. Talking about the patient as "the spleen in bed 9" or "the appendicitis in the corner", or in a maternity unit calling everyone "mother" removes individuality and thus protects the nurses and doctors from emotional demands. Life is especially hard for nurses on children's wards where the emotional demands can be overwhelming.

In any institution there is usually one person or group of workers who often catch the backlog of feelings not officially allowed. Janitorial staff, cleaners and domestics, and catering workers often pick up the real feelings from the public users of the organisation's services—and even from the professional staff themselves.

One group of workers who often catch unexpressed feelings in hospitals are physiotherapists. The whole process of massage involves yielding to another's care. It rouses far-off memories of infancy, of being handled and given comfort. It is not surprising that a high proportion of patients burst into tears as soon as the physiotherapist begins work. Sometimes the patient will talk, pouring out problems and anxieties, but just as often nothing is said and tears slowly subside into relaxation. Some physiotherapists have intuitively incorporated this response into their work.

In one Scottish psychiatric hospital I know, the nursing staff have learned to refer patients with whom they are failing to communicate to the physiotherapist. These are patients cut off from their capacity to feel, presumably to protect themselves from emotional pain. Frequently when they feel the physiotherapist's hands on them they will begin to cry. The massage is not stopped, even to produce a handkerchief, and no reference is made to the cause of the tears. Before the patient leaves the physiotherapist uses a particular technique to help work through the big sobs that so often follow crying. Before the patients go back to the ward, they will pat their faces back into place and often ask for reassurance that no one will be told. This is a desperate comment on the forbidden nature of tears.

Social workers and chaplains with a hospital office, also offer opportunities for a few patients to express distress in privacy, in a sympathetic atmosphere. But important though these opportunities are to individuals, they are marginal to the life of the hospital. One most distressing aspect of most institutions is the lack of privacy. If you're a patient on a ward, where can you cry? There is no place you can be quiet with a partner or a friend. About the only place is the lavatory and in the lavatory you cry alone. And a natural innocent expression of feeling becomes sullied and distorted. When respect is not given to our tears we are denied the relief they can bring.

We know that the patient who can show distress about their condition, talk about it and share anxiety has a much faster recovery rate than one who has to suppress such feelings. Alexander the Great is recorded as having some intuition of this. Having himself been wounded in the thigh, he walked round his wounded men and asked each to talk about what happened in the battle and how each man's wound had been received. This is particularly the case for patients undergoing operations. The work of psychiatrists like Maxwell Jones some years ago showed that the nurse who is given time to talk with and listen to patients is a most potent healing force for the human spirit.

These practices are being used in marvellous ways in hospices for the dying. They offer great hope and these understandings of human need to be transferred to general hospitals and other institutions.

chapter twelve
Bricks of shame

But there is no sleep when men must weep
who never yet have wept.

Oscar Wilde
The Ballad of Reading Gaol

Sometimes, when driving through a strange place, usually on the outskirts of a town, I see a building immediately recognisable as a prison. As I look, I half expect to see the air above the building turbulent and violent with the compressed energy of the pain and anger held inside. Prisons are terrible places. Prisons, perhaps more than any other institution, give a barometer reading of the state of civilisation in any society. They are like a living record of how we measure up in considering the needs of others. No matter how they are dressed up, modernised or staffed by well-meaning people, there is not a single prison in Britain that we can or should be proud of.

Though it seems necessary for some, there can be nothing positive about locking people up. It is made clear to the prisoner from the moment he sets foot in the institution that personal feelings are considered irrelevant. He is given a number, stripped of all possessions, made to shower and wash his hair with a lice-killing soap and then given uniform clothing. He has to respond like a well-trained dog to demands shouted at him. The small cubicle in which the new prisoner has had traditionally to strip, hand over his own clothes and put on prison uniform is known as the "dog box".

No matter what difficulties he encounters within the system, he can expect no sympathy. His progress is assessed on his ability to respond promptly and without feeling to whatever is asked.

Prisons as we know them are fairly modern institutions. In earlier times an offender might be banished, mutilated or hanged. Prisons were only used to hold a few people until trial. Now they hold tens of thousands.

Every process of the criminal justice system, even before a sentence is passed and guilt or innocence established, is designed to deny the person being held. On sentence the process is intensified. The object seems to be for the institution to establish, as quickly as possible, its power over the prisoner. This was shown in its most brutal form in a report published following riots in an Australian prison. An initiation ritual had been established for prisoners where for the first week officers were encouraged to beat and humiliate the arrival in nauseous ways. Only after his spirit had been broken did the brutality ease up. He was then considered "manageable".

This kind of procedure, or milder forms of it, may work with the majority. But the marvellous thing about human beings is that there is always someone in any group who will not be crushed or defeated. We applaud this kind of person when they climb mountains, cross deserts, sail oceans and survive against incredible odds. It is precisely the same quality that makes some people resist brutality or self-denying routines in prisons. But we do not applaud that. In the Australian prison the prisoners set their buildings on fire which led to the enquiry and the report. One Australian judge, a passionate advocate of the human spirit, has a photograph of the prison burning hanging on his office wall. He says it reinforces his faith in human beings.

As far as the institution is concerned, the ideal prisoner is not an individual person with feelings and needs but someone who will follow orders immediately, eat when he's told to, work, take exercise, sleep and all in ways respectful to authority. Preferably the prisoner should not show any feelings.

Almost the only feeling considered "respectable" for male prisoners is anger. Anger is understood in these all-male institutions by both staff and prisoners. Within limits, they are all comfortable with it. Subservience is also shown because other prisoners see it as a mask, necessary for survival for weaker or less competent prisoners. Away from staff, the subservient prisoner will say what he really thinks. No one will cry openly.

The prison hero is the one who most openly shows anger and contempt for the staff. Equally, the most brutal and aggressive member of staff is often most admired by the inmates as well as being most deeply hated. Staff and inmates meet in a culture of machismo, of men being tough. Normally senior staff have become separated from this but their own experience in the ranks leaves them fully aware of the emotional dynamics. Occasionally they are unable to leave them behind.

One story now in the mythology of the prison service concerns a governor who granted an interview to a prisoner but rather summarily refused his request. He was suddenly attacked by the prisoner with a knife specially sharpened for the purpose. The officers guarding him stopped him reaching the governor just in time. Instead of putting him on a charge, the governor took the knife out of his hand and while the prisoner was still being held by the officers, slashed his face. It was done, so the story goes, coolly and without malice. The governor became a hero to many of his staff and prisoners, including the one slashed. They admired him even as they reviled him. Psychologically there may be little difference between the personalities of some staff and prisoners. Their different paths can seem as much the result of luck, accident or opportunity as any capacity to distinguish between right and wrong.

Since prisoners and staff live in a climate where anger is the only respected emotional currency, it becomes very difficult for genuine feelings of distress or even sorrow to be expressed A frequent comment of observers about a prisoner who has committed a serious offence like murder is that he shows no remorse. This is of course, important when the staff are writing reports for the parole board. A desperate prisoner, knowing perfectly well what is expected of him, may well offer to a chaplain or prison visitor any amount of repentance. He might even take on a religious conversion. But the prisoner who feels integrity and a sense of loyalty to his own group, although he may sincerely repent his crime, might find it impossible to express this publicly. The whole atmosphere discourages the sharing of personal feelings.

But to express feelings or even cry in a setting that allows no privacy is difficult. The majority share a cell. Not even toileting is private. A phone message may have come to say that a parent has died, a letter saying that a wife is seeking divorce, but there is nowhere to hide and be alone with sorrow. Indeed, prisoners are not allowed to display tender feelings under any circumstances.

This denial of feeling is in any case, well established in prisoners. A very high proportion come from a background of grossly limited educational and economic opportunity. Before reaching the status of adult prisoner, many have trod a path of minor delinquency and many have spent time as children in residential care. These junior institutions are the preparatory schools of the prisons, not because they train criminals but because they train youngsters to cope with a regime that denies tenderness, warmth and the right to weep for your own pain.

This style fits too well into the values and expectations

most will have encountered from male relatives and heroes. "Real men" don't show feelings, especially feelings of tenderness or tearfulness in public. What is allowed is sentimentality in drunken songs of nationality and ideal love. Mawkish videos are legitimate triggers for a show of feeling.

In prisons that offer art or creative writing classes, inmates will pour out their frustrated feelings in painting or poetry. But this kind of work is seen as marginal to the work of the prison instead of being seized as a central opportunity to reawaken feelings that have been buried. Instead of prison being used, as it could be for those who have to be there, as a living and learning opportunity about human relationships, prisoners live in a place where it is dangerous to let your feelings be seen because they can be used against you. Hostile staff or fellow prisoners are known to use the technique of "winding you up" to force a display of feeling, which is then ridiculed or punished.

Each experience of imprisonment, for even the most hardened recidivist, is a wrenching of the spirit. Except for those few unhappy souls who are grateful to have all choice removed from their lives, each person who hears the prison door clang feels a desolation at being cut off from the world. Sadness at the loss and anger against those who have deprived them of their liberty war within the soul. Sadness can't be shown. The fact that you're frightened can't be shown. If you show it you're finished, without respect from your peers and always an underdog. The prisoner learns in this jungle to trust no one. You never know when feelings will be used against you.

Those who suffer most are the prisoners who allow their mask to sink through all the layers of their personality and blot out the warm, loving, sorrowing parts of themselves. They will say that they don't have the courage to stay emotionally alive, particularly if they are serving a long sentence. Some refuse to allow visits from their wives. They will say they don't want letters, to be reminded of birthdays, nor sent a Christmas card. They would rather play dead than face the pain of thinking about their wives and family and the ordinary small activities of family life that they didn't value enough when they had freedom.

There are other pains too, such as celibacy. Outside people talk about prisoners missing physical sex. The need for conjugal visits is discussed by some as if the prisoners were just animals who needed relief from tension. It is true that most prisoners miss sexual contact but not just to get relief. Masturbation is freely practised even in cells shared by three men and usually homosexual encounters are possible. But the real loss is not genital sex but the small intimacies that freedom makes possible . . . the hugging, the kissing, the cuddling, the skin contact, the smell not only of their partner but of their children after a bath.

And there is the pain of jealousy. The agony of lying locked in a cell and wondering what your wife or girlfriend is doing. Imagination runs riot. Memories of one's own lovemaking are replayed with another man playing your part. Carrying these thoughts, the partner's visit can turn into a nightmare. How much easier to cut yourself off from all of these problems and withdraw emotionally into the less demanding machine of prison life. One prisoner put it like this. "I waken up every morning with this pain. It's terrible. It's not that I want to die, but I just want to get out of my mind." He means this literally.

It is this wanting to get out of one's mind that creates such a strong demand for drugs. Drugs in prison ease the pain, creating a private world of peace into which the prisoner can withdraw and forget the awfulness. Some who are distressed in a way that can be judged as illness are given drugs officially. These tend to be prisoners who are a problem for the discipline staff, either excessively violent or suicidal. Suicides in prison are administratively very tedious, so to avoid the risk drugs become a way for personal issues to be avoided. Violence can be interpreted as paranoia and that makes drugging an acceptable way of handling the behaviour without having to examine the prisoner's circumstances or anything in the prison system that might be causing the violent behaviour. The rest of the prisoners have to rely on drugs being smuggled in occasionally by visitors as a gift or by prison staff.

There are a number of young prisoners who are so cut off from their feelings that they have no fear and no sense of compassion. They don't even have anger. The offences that brought them into prison tend to be extremely cold-blooded. They feel nothing about seriously mutilating someone for a trivial reason. When in prison they blackmail staff with threats to their family and children if not supplied with drugs. This apparent lack of feeling is, in every case, reinforced by the prison way of life.

When any expression of intimacy is impossible, it has to be withdrawn. Even visits have to be conducted in the babble of a large hall or though glass or wire. No one can go on yearning indefinitely for what is not available. In male prisons, while homosexual relationships exist they are less likely to be tolerated if they involve truly loving feelings. A "hard" man may have a strong homosexual aspect to his personality that can only be indulged in prison. But it can only be demonstrated as a power relationship in the taking by force of young attractive prisoners.

When sexual tenderness is denied it is replaced by crudity and pornography. Cell walls are covered with fantasy women, always available, pouting and meaningless, two-dimensional figures, there for any kind of degradation and brutality you want to inflict. The only kind of conversation about women permitted is crude and obscene but in a strange way this is a bridge between the prisoners and the staff who share these attitudes. The prison landing office is sometimes decorated inside the cupboards with unusually squalid pornography.

When prisoners are released and return home, the institutional defences cannot easily be given up. Yet it is impossible for an ordinary woman, perhaps with two or three young children, or by now middle-aged, to live up to the sexual fantasies built up within the containing cell. The reality is often a disappointment that cannot be discussed. Since for many men sexual capacity lies at the root of self-esteem, the ex-prisoner may try to find another woman to reassure him. An encounter without real warmth, without loving feelings, but exciting in its strangeness, may help achieve his climax within the woman but will only reinforce the message of prison that life is simpler without feelings.

By creating and maintaining systems that deny feelings of warmth and tenderness, by encouraging male competitive and aggressive styles of human encounter, prisons are killing off those qualities most likely to re-establish people in the community. These systems also damage prison staff. Simple social skills like apologising are given no place because the most important thing is not to lose face. Yet I have seen innumerable jobs lost by ex-prisoners because one morning they came in late and when challenged couldn't give a simple explanation and express regret. Instead they bridled, told employers to stuff their jobs and walked out, cursing themselves.

It is often said about notorious criminals that they have no feelings. This could be turned on its head. It may be that they have feelings stronger than law-abiding people, which is why they have committed crimes. From infancy they may have wanted more than they were given. They may have needed more—more love, more attention, more education, more stimulation, more explanation about the world they found themselves in. The corrective institution should not deny these needs even more drastically but offer, at no matter how late a date, opportunities. Instead of taking what they need or taking the shortfall out on others by theft, rape or murder, some might find more creative ways of asking.

chapter thirteen
Tears & grief

He that conceals his grief finds no remedy for it.
Turkish proverb

In 1989, at the Hillsborough football ground in Sheffield, England a normal Saturday afternoon sporting occasion was transformed, just minutes after the cup match between Liverpool and Nottingham Forest got underway, from a joyous boisterous spectacle into a disaster. At the now infamous Leppings Lane end of the ground allocated to Liverpool fans, a mighty surge in the crowd led to the deaths of ninety five supporters.

This was a massive human tragedy for the deceased, the many more injured, all the bereaved families, everyone else at the ground that day, and everyone connected with the game of football.

As far as the grieving process for this awful tragedy was

concerned, the Liverpool mourners were in one respect at least, fortunate. Weeping alone is painful. Like walking alone in dark places, a deep forest, or even deserted city streets, unanswered questions grow bigger and more terrible in the mind. In a state of shock and loss, we need something, someone, anything familiar to hold onto for reassurance. The big question Why? threatens to render all of life, all that we know and hold dear, meaningless.

It is maybe no coincidence that the Liverpool supporters' song is "You'll never walk alone". The city, with its long history of communal grief in the collective memory of Irish immigrants and their ancestors and desperate experiences of migration and unemployment, knew instinctively how to behave.

There was no attempt to hide the grief. It exploded, raw and naked. It was powered, as so much grieving is, not just by the disaster that triggered it, but by community memories of other griefs. Ordinary life was halted to allow time for the sorrow to penetrate the layers of defence that we all set up to blunt the pain of loss. Rituals showed honour and reverence for the dead. From the traditional laying of flowers to the weaving of scarves and colours into the fences of the club's Anfield stadium, the death and the loss was lent an intimate yet at the same time public meaning.

John Sweeney, writing in the *Observer* on the Sunday a week after the disaster, described "the shrine" created at the stadium:

Their faces tell the story. Some weep publicly; others walk high up into the stands and sob quietly. Still others are there to show their sympathy and respect, but also to see for themselves the spectacle of a city's mass grief.

And after a week, when the football ground had acted as a family home visited by friends from near and far in what was a traditional wake, the flowers and mementoes were ritually burned. Then the more intimate funerals took place, the city began to return to normal and grieving continued at a more private level. The private sense of loss, while inevitably painful, had been given meaning and dignity by the first experience of community support.

In a highly individualised society, we forget that grief has always been communal. Where people have value as group members, our lives are not only our own or just our immediate families'. In one sense they belong to the whole community, therefore each death is a loss to everyone. A public show of grief acknowledges that fact.

Since the earliest times religious rituals have surrounded death, the disposal of the body and the grieving process. In Judaism the bereaved person must be surrounded with friends and relatives in the first weeks and cared for. The Roman Catholic wake has served the same purposes. Protestantism brought more impersonal social conventions for the bereaved, emphasising behaviour rather than feelings, but continued to provide a strong framework within which grief could be experienced.

We do in fact, know a tremendous amount about the experience of loss and how vital it is as a primary human experience. Small children separated from their parents by war, death or illness go through desperate reactions of feeling which end in apathy and a sense of helplessness. These reactions, if not responded to by alternative caring adults, can lead to an inability to thrive physically and serious problems of mental health in later life. Even children separated for short periods of time can react with grief and anger followed by apathy. They can even appear not to recognise their parent when they return home. It is this knowledge that has led to more humane visiting hours in hospitals and provision for parents to stay with their children when they have to be admitted for serious conditions.

In adults, depending on the suddenness of the death and the relationship with the deceased, the first two to four weeks after a death are marked by shock, numbness and denial. The next six to eighteen months are the most painful. Here there are frequent reruns of the death, constant attempts to make sense of it and anger at having been abandoned by the dead person interspersed with the acute pain of loss. There can also be a kind of sanctification of the dead person. The dead partner is now seen as perfect no matter how awful he or she may have been in real life. These are all normal aspects of grieving.

For anything up to two years after a death, 10% to 20% of widows can still be considered to be clinically depressed but after this normally comes a time of reorganisation. Grief work, successfully completed, means letting go of the bonds that tie you to the dead person, forming new relationships as a single person and adjusting to a new identity and environment. The less traumatic the experience of loss in childhood the more successful will be the grief work inevitably faced in adult life.

Religious belief in an after life can help some people but we seem to know only a little about how in our secular society we should try to support the grieving. With any grieving process—whether over the loss of a elderly parent after a long illness, the inexplicable cot death of an infant, a stillborn baby, the loss of employment, status, the sense of identity and belonging such as refugees lose, a family pet—no one comes through totally unscarred. The wound never fully heals. A bit of ourselves, in the shape of previous life and memory, is lost. We grieve for the loss of an ideal or a belief, for changes in our body, a place we've had to leave, even an illusion.

Even if something or some person we dislike is lost, grieving can be as important. For it is for ourselves and our own lost years that we grieve—years, happy or sad, that will not come again.

But the grief of bereavement is most usually linked to the death of someone close, like our parents. Even if you are sixty or seventy years old yourself when that finally happens, your relationship with the world changes. You are now at the head of the personal queue filing toward the inevitability of the grave.

None of us can conceive that we might die before our parents. They are the candle against the dark night, that protected us in our childhood. Now it is extinguished and we are alone in the dark. Your relationship with the world changes in another way. You are now a "man" or a "woman", rather than still being able at some level to think of yourself as a child. We take into ourselves aspects of our parents that we may have denied previously. We might become more like them in our styles and our habits. We might even begin to look at our children the way our parents looked at us. We might even assume that we will die at the age at which they died, and of the same disease or in the same way.

But reactions to parental death are not the same for everyone. My first reaction to my own mother's death was of relief. It took me a long time to admit that, but I gradually realised that many people were grateful to me for sharing that thought with them. It is more common than we realise.

Some relief came from having the burden of exhaustion lifted. My mother's last illness had been long and painful for her and emotionally and physically demanding for me. But then the whole of our relationship had been fraught with tension. Even when she was well, I had never been able to relax because I never knew from one day to the next how I was going to find her. Early in life she had managed to change roles with me so that I felt responsible for her, rather than she for me. It was only long after her death that I realised how much anger lay under my acceptance of that responsibility and how much energy I had used holding that down.

At first I couldn't let myself grieve. On the afternoon of the funeral, not knowing what to do with myself, I went to a cinema. It was practically empty. I sat in the front row of the balcony with tears rolling down my face and seeing nothing at all. My body was crying but my heart was empty. I couldn't let myself feel the pain until many years later and with the pain came anger.

No relationship is without conflict yet we rarely talk honestly about the faults of the person who has died. "Do not speak ill of the dead," we are told. Yet it is really a great comfort to be with a friend who shares knowledge of how awful the dead person could sometimes be. Ministers, priests and those taking secular funerals, instead of just eulogising the deceased, would more helpfully present a realistic rather than an idealised picture. Some national newspapers have begun, in their obituary columns, to acknowledge that their subjects, no matter how distinguished, have been like the rest of us still living, part saint and part sinner.

The Glasgow physician and therapist, Cameron Macdonald in his book on psychosomatic illness writes about some of the health implications of grief reactions that are not dealt with. He talks about the importance of recognising the three Rs that dominate our responses—Regret, Reproach and Relief. We regret the things we failed to do; we reproach ourselves for the things we did do; and we feel relief that it's over and we can move on. An inability to move through these feelings with some gentleness to ourselves, he shows, can result in unresolved grief and even illness.

In Britain we have lost many rituals that in the past supported us through the various stages of grief. We no longer wear mourning clothes for a fixed period of time. We don't refuse to go to parties for the first six months after the death of someone close. We don't take time immediately after the death for a intensive grieving. As a result we don't give signals to our friends and neighbours to sympathise in obvious ways.

On the contrary we openly challenge the old rituals. We turn up to funerals in everyday clothes. We refuse to let people send flowers so there is no chance for a communal expression of feeling. We are reluctant to take more than one day off work on the grounds that we're better getting on with life as if weeping and mourning had no part in real life. Worse, we give no signals to *ourselves* that we need time to grieve. We abandon the support of formal steps that move us out of that grief back into loving life.

The funeral ritual is particularly important in providing an end point. Even in the Lockerbie disaster, where a plane exploded in mid air and many bodies could only be pieced together in fragments, relatives came from the other side of the world searching for something, anything that gave a focus to their grief and over which they could weep. Terrible problems arise for survivors of death at sea or explosions where not even fragments are left. One group who suffer deeply are secret, adulterous lovers where the partner is killed and the survivor is unable to see the body or go to the funeral. Sometimes they are unable to tell any other human being of their loss.

The relatives of those who commit suicide face great conflicts. They are expected by friends and neighbours to follow the normal passages of grieving, yet often they are consumed with anger. It is as if the dead person had killed themselves to get away from them or as a punishment. The act of suicide among young people is indeed often an act of anger against those they live with.

Some people seem to stage their suicides in ways that punish the survivor. I knew one family where the husband hung himself facing the front door so that his body would be the first thing his wife would see as she came in. The mixture of anger and guilt that overwhelmed his widow made it impossible for her to grieve and weep for the loss of the good things shared in the early days of their marriage.

For the children of suicides there is an equal if not greater burden to bear. At some level every child is aware of being their parent's future. By committing suicide the parent is rejecting what they offer. The parent has turned aside from pride and pleasure in their child. They have withdrawn any investment in their future, such as the joy of potential grandchildren. How can a child or young person grieve in sorrow for someone who denies their existence in that way? There are many layers of hurt to peel off before they can see their parent as a human being seeking a way out of a private torment.

In the dense undergrowth of mixed feelings that arise at a death, it is perhaps not surprising that other people's responses to the bereaved is awkward and embarrassed. Other people's grief stirs our own unshed tears. Because there are so few rituals to handle this confusion of feeling, friends may avoid us, even by crossing to the other side of the street. Part of this might come from a superstitious but unacknowledged feeling that grief is contagious and unlucky. The bereaved are dimly aware of these feelings and are equally embarrassed about displaying tears. They can avoid their friends or hide signs of distress, not wanting to be a "nuisance". A nameless sense of guilt accompanies some bereaved, as if they are mysteriously to blame.

Women traditionally show their grief more than men. This makes it more likely they will be avoided. This can include a reluctance to ask them to visit or to come for a meal, or even the fear felt by some women that a grieving woman may attract their own husbands. Grieving men are easier to deal with. It is acceptable to ask them over for a meal—they are not expected to manage without a caring woman. They arouse protectiveness in women and are not seen as a threat by other men.

One profession that sees more of the bereaved than the rest of us are undertakers. Perhaps twenty times a week each one has to confront a dead body. They have to meet, talk with and help relatives and friends cope with the practical arrangements posed by the death. No matter what the feelings of the bereaved, the body has to be got out of the way. All other creatures on earth leave the dead bodies of their own kind to rot in the open air. Only humans have devised complicated rituals that convey mystery and respect, along with mourning and tears.

The code of practice of the Association of Funeral Directors describes every step of their procedures for dealing with a dead body but constantly emphasises the need to behave with respect, the need to act "as if the next of kin were standing at their elbow, or act as if the deceased were a member of their own family." We all recognise how important these conventions are. For those of us who, after the Second World War, sat riveted to cinema screens as we watched the opening up of the concentration camps, watched the piled-up heaps of dead bodies, our whole perception of civilised behaviour was outraged. It was a fundamental assault on our sensibility and aroused a horror almost too deep for tears.

But the equally necessary professional detachment of undertakers gives them a valuable view of human reactions. They see the range of responses from deep and bitter grief to awkward attempts to simulate grief where it no longer has relevance for the relationship.

The first reaction to the death of someone important to us is usually disbelief, just as to news of our own impending death. The human psyche finds the idea of its own destruction intolerable and another's death can be a threat to our fantasies of immortality. Disbelief comes even when death has been expected, but is most acute when death is sudden.

It is as if we go into a state of shock to protect us from the knowledge. A kind of numbness acts as a shell against not only the death itself, but against all the implications of loss that go with it. Occasionally the shell cracks, awareness creeps in and normally tears and weeping come. When the pain becomes intolerable, the numbness and disbelief take over again to protect us. The cycle keeps repeating. At this stage you are normally expected to experience grief when the main feeling is shock. Real grief comes later—only then are you ready to share your deep suffering. People in contact with the bereaved (and the bereaved themselves) find this time-lag disconcerting. The grief can be displaced and a man unable to cry at his father's funeral may find himself weeping for days three months later when his spaniel is run over.

But the story is unfinished. Another normal step in the process of grieving, one that follows closely on numbness, is anger—often just a free-floating general sort of anger that lasts until around the anniversary of the death that provoked it. This is often the feeling the bereaved find most difficult to acknowledge—their anger against the dead person for abandoning them to face the world alone.

Rationality is irrelevant here. Under our sophisticated social exteriors, our needs are quite simple. When we were small our loved parents would sometimes leave us when we didn't want them to. We were bereft. We didn't understand the good reasons why they couldn't be with us. All we knew was that they were not there when we needed them. And we blamed them. Why shouldn't we have? And old habits die hard. Scratch any one of us and you will find a small child. The loss of anyone close and deeply loved rouses the same feelings of anger.

In the acute period following on from a loss, this anger can turn us in all kinds of unpredictable directions. In the confusion, both men and women may turn to a friend or even a stranger for a sexual encounter—often to the scandal of friends and neighbours. Few people try to understand how, if the bereaved truly loved their now dead partner, they can behave in such a "shameless" way. Yet it is because they loved their partner so deeply that they are driven to seek ways of easing their pain, fear and anger.

One middle-aged woman whose husband died suddenly of a heart attack reacted in a storm of sexual behaviour with a succession of younger men. Her family was scandalised because she made no effort to hide what she was doing. She herself was amazed by her own actions and between episodes was bitterly ashamed of what was happening to her. For about fifteen months after her husband's death she was driven into these encounters.

She came out of the need quite suddenly one afternoon when, after sex, her partner held her tenderly. None of the others has done this and she began to cry. Not the angry resentful tears she'd cried after her husband's death, but like a small child seeking comfort. Fortunately the man was able to let her weep and talk about the pain. After this experience she was celibate for about three years. Later she married a man of about her own age, in many ways like her former husband. She can now talk about her anger at being suddenly deserted and see that her behaviour was a shouted defiance at the world she no longer felt able to trust.

Anger against the person who has died can be experienced as dangerous and may not be tolerated by the wider society or by the bereaved themselves. So other outlets for our anger and sense of loss have to be found.

And it is not always realised that the pain of loss is experienced physically as well as mentally. Many people can point to the part of their bodies where the pain is felt and to ease it, many diversions are tried. Some women attack their own bodies, scratching and tearing at their own skin until the blood runs. They tug at their hair, pull it out at the roots, roll around the floor and bang their heads against the wall. The physical pain brings a temporary sense of relief. All of these activities are also seen in the behaviour of children grossly neglected and deprived of affection and attention.

Other people turn their anger outwards. Doctors and hospitals are a good target—"they should be made to pay!" The man driving the other car "should go to prison for life". The murderer should be hung! After the Hillsborough football disaster, within a week we heard accusations against the police, against the clubs, against the fans themselves who were accused of being drunk and causing trouble. In seeking revenge, we seek to rid ourselves of pain. Our lives are miserable as we remember times when we might have been kinder, we might have been more loving, less impatient. We wake up during the night with desperate thoughts of what horrible people we are and with feelings of guilt that we are alive and the loved one is dead.

Some people get stuck at this point. They move backward and forward between denial and anger and depression, unable to break out of the circle of despair. They are unable to enter into a total experience of mourning where they acknowledge the loss and pain without needing to deny it or blame anyone.

We all know widows and widowers who have failed to recover from loss, whose family or friends can find no way of breaking into their misery and inevitably become tired of trying. It is often partners who have been most able to express their feelings who are most likely to cope with bereavement and make friendships anew.

With any loss, because at some level our very integrity and identity as individuals are shaken, we have to go through what has been termed "the dark night of the soul". Tears in time will ease both our physical and emotional pain. One woman described how she had gone back to work after the death of her husband, determined to be brave. She kept maniacally busy so as not to feel sorrow and set herself the goal of working so hard that at night she fell into bed exhausted. She would wake in the night hearing sobs, then realise they were hers and then stop.

After some weeks, instead of taking a sleeping pill she decided to lie awake and feel what her body was telling her. She began to think of her husband and how much she missed having the comfort of his body in bed. She began to cry deep gut-wrenching sobs, more painful than anything she had ever known. They went on for three hours before she fell asleep, exhausted but more relaxed than since her husband died. She said later that it was the same kind of relaxation the body feels after a really satisfying orgasm, every muscle relaxed and a marvellous sense of peace.

She stayed off work the next morning and for the rest of

the week. She stayed at home, weeping intermittently but never again with the same passion and desperation of that first outburst. She went over the whole experience of first meeting her husband, their courtship and marriage and life together. She talked to friends, not only about the happy times they'd had together but about the inevitable disappointments. She faced her anger at being abandoned at an earlier age than anyone would have expected, and talked about loneliness. Hour after hour, the thoughts she had been pushing back came pouring out.

Weak, but feeling as she put it, "lighter", she returned to work. She was able to warn her manager that for a while she might be a bit slower and occasionally a bit tearful. Her colleagues were relieved that the tense, frantic performance given since her husband's death had stopped. They hadn't known how to get through to her and were happy to give support.

Each of us brings to grieving everything else that has happened in our lives. Somewhere in our heads we carry every grief experienced and in any new loss, each comes to life again. If as children we were given healing opportunities to grieve for a range of losses—from falling and losing our balance, to the death of a cat, from losing a favourite doll, to moving house, we will have learned an inner sense of security that will give strength during later losses.

Many children are not helped. "Don't be silly", "don't make such a fuss" are the messages from parents who don't appreciate the intensity of children's grief. When parents exclude children from their own grief it can make the child feel that the awful event that has taken place is a punishment for which they are in part responsible. The parents' intention is often to protect so they hide tears and sorrow by putting on a ghastly pretence of cheerfulness. Yet a child who has lost its father by death or divorce is not helped by a mother who denies her own sadness.

One young woman whose husband was killed in an air crash described how all her friends had said she musn't cry in front of her six year old daughter. They said she must stay cheerful for the child's sake. So she saved her tears until she was in bed. After about two years she met a man and fell in love. Although concerned that her daughter had stayed very withdrawn from this new partner, she agreed to marry. It was when she told the girl of her marriage plans that the little girl's feelings came out. She said, "You're glad Daddy died, aren't you!" She had assumed that because her mother hadn't wept or shown grief that her father hadn't been loved by anyone but herself and her father's parents who had wept copiously.

Ironically the mother had been supporting the grandparents in their grief, while hiding her own. Her daughter's attack made her break down and weep and after they'd cried together they talked about the misunderstandings. The mother postponed her second marriage for six months to give time to sort out the new relationships, to grieve the past and plan for the future.

For a parent to hide sorrow or even anger denies the child's right to have their own feelings Our grief is our own and no one has the right to take it away. It always reclaims us. Unresolved mourning has the power to erupt as an overwhelming crisis when a further loss happens. Not only a death, but any loss, like redundancy or retirement, that shakes one's sense of purpose.

chapter fourteen
Weeping for the world

"I'm frightened if I let out the pain it will destroy me," he said and burst into tears.

There are some people who openly weep for the threats our world faces. They are thought of as eccentrics rather than prophets. Most commonly fears about the state of the world are expressed in private. They can follow on from an experience of mystery or beauty like the birth of a baby, or the day an infant takes her first steps, or being moved by the scenery from the top of a mountain. Things that are a source of joy seem to bring out a reverse sadness that they can so easily be destroyed. We are after all, ourselves mortal. So other joyous beautiful things must be finite and considerations of war, famine, oppression, pollution or holocaust which might bring about a premature end to joy are a cause for tears.

There are parents who wake weeping with nightmares

of seeing their children incinerated in a nuclear war. Newspapers and t.v. bring us immediate first-hand accounts of the human costs of war and famine. We are assailed daily with detailed information about the destruction of the rain forests, about acid rain, nuclear waste, the hole in the ozone layer. We are given information as if somehow knowing the facts will force us to do something. Some people get out their cheque books, others stuff a fiver into an envelope, but most of us can only say, "Isn't that terrible!" and feel helpless as if it's all too much to believe.

But taking pain out of the privacy and secrecy of the individual heart into the world can change it—and change things in the world. Yet what politicians in power fear most is the expression of strong feelings by members of the public except, that is, for feelings that they themselves inspire and feel able to control, like patriotism and party loyalty. For the state, the ideal citizen is modest, sober, hardworking, thrifty and moderate in all his views. Just as it was to our parents when we yelled with distress, public passion is unacceptable and suspect.

But sometimes it is difficult to avoid certain truths and the feelings they arouse. Every country has a significant group of people who live their suffering daily. They are not all landless peasants in economically "underdeveloped" countries. Many are urban poor living in poverty in the midst of an affluent society, a group which has come to be known as the Fourth World.

In London, where shops sell children's party dresses costing more than the average weekly wage, many children are undernourished and living desperate lives in bed-and-breakfast hostels because their parents can find no decent jobs and housing. In Glasgow, designated European City of Culture in 1990, poverty caused by lack of jobs rots human lives. Desolate housing estates drag down the human spirit so that energy that could go into work and positive living experiences deteriorates into vandalism, querulousness, jealousy, loss of dignity and self respect. Family life is permeated by anxiety about every aspect of daily routines—the buying of food, the heating of the home, the care of children, the future of young people.

Attempts to work together to improve things can be destroyed by the weight of tension and stress people carry daily. One community worker said, "People bring the stress that they're living in into a committee. So they "fuck and blind" and go back home to stress as well." They go back to fighting with their husbands or with their children. The middle class have a support network; the poor have only a sense of helplessness.

It is maybe not surprising that in poor areas little attention seems to be able to be paid to the wider suffering that goes on in the world. If your heart is full of a sense of bitter injustice, if the area where you live is polluted by neglected housing, public squalor, vandalism and drug peddling, it is hard to focus on what goes on in far-flung places. If the only world you know is physically ugly, how can you weep for the loss of beauty? If every time you watch television you are reminded by adverts, documentaries and soap operas of your isolation and exclusion from the wider society, it is difficult to maintain a sense of the wholeness and interconnectedness of the planet.

In a society that glorifies individual achievement and competition, people often blame themselves if they fail. No one wants to display their poverty so social contact shrinks between unemployed families and those still in jobs. Both groups are embarrassed. How can you enjoy showing holiday snaps from Ibiza to a friend who hasn't been able to do more than take the children to the local park for a picnic? The affluent therefore avoid the poor. They don't want to feel guilty and conclude in self-defence that it's their own fault they're unemployed. "Surely," they will say, "they can do something to help themselves."

The unemployed will also avoid the affluent as their lives seem to become increasingly shameful in their own eyes, unable as they are to keep up patterns of buying clothes, going out for an occasional meal or standing someone a drink in a pub. They do not like their own feelings of resentment. Such feelings reinforce a sense of failure and increase feelings of helplessness and powerlessness.

What makes us human is our capacity to understand our own feelings. But in the face of the inequalities and injustices that we see daily in our society, we choose not to use that capacity and by example teach our children not to. If anything, we teach them to ignore these awkward feelings. So we should not be surprised if some people living under the stress of poverty, especially the young, will express feelings of anger and frustration. But since they cannot seem to get to the true causes of their stress, they just turn to vandalism, gang fighting and petty crime.

If fighting back seems impossible or unacceptable, as it is to most women, the old and the more cautious members of the community, people simply take flight. Television becomes the main source of stimulation to "pass the time". At any time, day or night, in street after street of dreary housing estates, the flickering light can be seen reflected through the windows. People isolate themselves, only venturing out when absolutely necessary. They are taking flight from the pain of their lives.

Another place to flee is inside your own head—in wishful thinking, day dreaming, or into a bottle or jar of pills. For others who try to avoid such sedative solutions, illness may be a respectable alternative. Feelings of fear, anger, despair are denied. And because the capacity to feel is indivisible, people get to the stage that they hardly feel anything at all. Even positive, cooperative and loving feelings are lost to them.

Stein Ringen, in his book *The Possibility of Politics*, describes research showing that the more prosperous a community, the more likely people are to take part in social and political life. Other research shows that such confident groups are also more likely to have the capacity to draw on a range of emotions, none of which totally overwhelms them. They can be angry while still holding on to reason. They can be unhappy and weep without feeling suicidal. They can stumble and fail and then pick themselves up again. For anyone living under constant stress, as are people in chronic poverty, the considered response is harder to achieve. If results are not immediate, there is no hope. Good and bad are more sharply defined. All previous experience makes trust risky.

The fact is that groups of people who live in even a modest degree of affluence are able to buy themselves out of a number of anxieties. Going somewhere with small children is a much simpler operation if everyone can bundle into the car, and waterproofs thrown into the boot just in case it rains. The alternative of getting coats on to sometimes resistant small bodies, walking to the bus stop carrying bags, waiting, getting children and pushchair on to the bus, keeping them happy on a crowded bus and after reaching the destination knowing you have to go through the whole thing in reverse is exhausting for anyone. If you're also short of money, you're driven to the edge of toleration. Then tearful children, reacting possibly to the parent's stress, are more likely to be slapped than comforted.

And this is only one of a whole range of situations where money makes life simpler—like paying for help to clean the house and do the ironing; being able to afford good-quality prepared foods and well-designed clothes; employing baby-sitters who make relaxation and adult contact possible.

These examples relate to parents of young children, one of the most highly stressed groups in any community, but the same applies to people who are elderly and disabled and those caring for them . . . in fact, to any human being. The financial ability to use taxis, phones, restaurants, dry cleaners, etc, etc offers a way of buying out of stress. They are especially important for women who hold the responsibility and the anxiety for so much of the detail of living.

In communities where distress and suffering are the rule, weeping is not readily available as a release. For one thing, the roles of men and women are more sharply defined. For the public face men are tough and macho in style, women submissive. In the private face, women are strong and coping; men like an extra child in the family but with special privileges. It seems impossible for the women to truly weep for their existential distress. They say they would never stop, so better not to start.

Since sorrow and pain lie constantly just beneath the surface for everyone, the danger is that weeping publicly provokes depression and anger rather than spontaneous and helpful shows of feeling.

Tears are often kept for matters unconnected with the real pain and alcohol is a common trigger. Under its influence strong men weep on each other's shoulders for the sorrows of the world, their country, city or football team. The women weep for their innocence. They thought life was going to be different. But as the pointlessness and ineffectiveness of sentimental tears to relieve the true source of pain become evident, the feeling shifts quickly to anger—not used in ways that can change lives, but turned against husbands, children or neighbours.

The social service departments find it very difficult to work in these communities. The "client" is almost invariably a woman, since it is women who are expected by their husbands to negotiate with the official world. This is another example of shifting the anxiety onto the least powerful. Social workers are also mostly women so in a majority of cases we have professional women managing poor women.

Conventional ways of working ignore the fact that most poor women are themselves brilliant managers of small amounts of money. They use skills of juggling, sharing, borrowing, postponing payment, then in the nick of time finding something extra—skills that would make them a fortune if their arena was the Stock Exchange rather than the local shops. And unlike the social worker who is advising them, they manage without credit cards or knowing they can have an overdraft if needed. In addition they negotiate and keep the peace in families with a grievous lack of space and comforts.

In encounters with social workers very little real weeping takes place. If it starts, the box of Kleenex is produced and a silent, urgent message passed—"Please don't cry. I really can't cope with that." This is probably true. If they let themselves be moved by the sorrows endured by the families of the poor they would have to weep with them. And what would happen then to the other seven families waiting to be seen?

But who is to say that it might not be the most loving and helpful thing to do? The worker's need to hold back tears simply confirms expectations of what to expect from authority. For the worker who holds out the Kleenex and says kindly but firmly, "Here, dry your eyes", it is another stone in the wall of defence against pain she is building round her heart.

Community workers don't expect people to weep. They understand very well the nature and intensity of the pain that exists in communities but have no way of dealing with it on an individual basis. They believe that group action is important, not individuals' responses. What they hope for is that individual pain, when shared, will generate anger and energy necessary to bring about change at a local and national level. What too often they fail to see is that creative rather than destructive responses to pain can only come when contact is consciously made with the sadness that underlies the anger. It is awareness of the underlying sadness of the human condition that links us to each other.

Meanwhile, for people living under the constant stress of poverty, the capacity to cope with the minutiae of daily life is reduced. Depression and anxiety are the most common responses for women, especially those with small children. Depression comes where there is a sense that nothing you can do, no amount of protest can bring about change. Anxiety comes when you never know where the next blow of fate is coming from and are always trying to dodge it. The only source of help is often the local doctor who tends, since he knows the stress and feels himself helpless, to give traditional mood-altering drugs.

Many women need ever increasing doses of tranquillisers and anti-depressants. One effect of these is to dry up their tears. Groups to help women overcome their dependency on these drugs find that rediscovering the ability to cry is one of the sure signs of the start of recovery. Men who take refuge from their depression or anxiety in a bottle are ignored until their liver collapses or they have delirium tremens. Psychological help it seems, is still widely seen as something for the middle classes who have problems that are "really" emotional rather than worries about how to pay an electricity bill.

There have been some attempts to confront and transform the pain of the community. Some of the most imaginative have emerged in Scotland. The Craigmillar Festival Society began in a desperately deprived Edinburgh housing scheme of that name. It was described as a festival in gentle but defiant guying of the prestigious international festival of music, drama and the arts that attracts big crowds, massive finance and wealthy patrons to Edinburgh every year.

Craigmillar is the kind of area where it is easier to put people in touch with community suffering than to confront the personal. The society was started by local women and Helen Crummy, who was the organiser for many years, has written of the importance of the arts, music, painting, poetry and drama as a means of expressing community suffering. Through that expression, bringing into consciousness the history of their own community, the local people recognised their own strengths. They became aware of their instinct for survival and the ways that they were able to weep, laugh and create life and joy out of the most unlikely situations. In celebrating these capacities through the arts they learnt how to transmute pain into creativity. Quickly the Festival Society widened its scope to provide all kinds of supportive services to individuals and tackled community development projects like schools, roads, transport, housing and job initiatives.

Other organisations have drawn inspiration from Craigmillar. The pain in the lives of people forced to live in the areas of deprivation has been dramatised, photographed, written and sung about. But so has their joy, their capacity to work in cooperation with others, their creativity. The first is recognised and respected and that makes possible the celebration of the second. To celebrate one's strengths is a liberating experience. It is the first step to self-respect.

Among many other global problems, the gross inequalities of wealth that exist both between countries and within countries like our own are the source of great pain. But whether rich or poor, we all have something in common, namely the human capacity to feel sorrow and anger, to own our pain. There is no society in which such feelings are not central. What separates us is the range of defences we use to protect ourselves from sorrow and pain.

Only by opening ourselves to the pain we know exists can we discover that far from being our enemy that we need to deny, its recognition can be our most powerful ally to alleviate it and change the circumstances that feed it. Only through contact with our own feelings of sorrow and sadness, owning our tears, can we find the route to our full humanity.

chapter fifteen
Tears, power and protest

He who has a why to live for can bear almost any how.
Nietzsche

Powerlessness and helplessness are among the most basic and destructive human experiences. We all know these feelings and depending on our previous histories they can arouse terror, anger or apathy. They can also provoke what is perhaps the most damaging defence mechanism of all—denial. We deny our real feelings.

But if we are aware of feeling put upon, or ignored, it can arouse our determination to challenge what is being done to us. We are born with the urge to protest and the potential for power. Direct protest, demanding that needs be met, is the meaning of the baby's first cry. It is a powerful message that proclaims the child's sense of her right to exist, take up space and be attended to. We demand that the pain of hunger be eased. We demand that the discomfort of our bodies be attended to. We demand to be held and nurtured.

Babies born without this capacity often die if they have to cope with an infection or the trauma of surgery. Doctors and nurses talk approvingly of children who struggle to survive. "She's a real fighter!" they'll say. The baby who thrusts hungrily for its mother's nipple is applauded and enjoyed. And when infant needs are met promptly and lovingly, a sense of power is born—a realisation that one is acknowledged, treated with respect, and that the cry of protest has produced results.

Later when words are put to feelings, "It's not fair!" is the passionate assertion that rings through childhood. "It's not fair!" has been the source of powerful human movements for freedom and justice.

So what goes wrong? Why are some babies not applauded and enjoyed, their demands not responded to, their needs secondary to the convenience of the adults caring for them? Why do some of us grow up to learn that we cannot influence or change our fate? What sometimes happens in growing up that turns some of us from creatures who battle to have our needs met, who shout and scream with frustration if our existence is denied, into apparently passive, disinterested adults, reluctant to confront issues and use energy creatively?

In addressing these kinds of questions it is of course

acknowledged that to some extent the growing person must change A sense of cooperation is needed, of sharing, an appreciation of others' needs and of delaying satisfying one's own needs. And of course, timing is important. Just at what stage the child is ready to learn responsibilities that can be taken into adult life is an important aspect to the process of growth. All this is accepted. It is the base on which these social responsibilities are laid that needs discussion here.

The fact is that the daily lives of infants and young children often erode their initial feelings of power. They are picked up and put down; they are fed, often when it suits the adult rather than the child; they are bathed and changed at times that can bear no relation to their needs. They are passed from one adult to another like parcels, without consultation; they are put to bed at times that suit the household rather than their need to sleep. They are expected, if girls, to kiss without making a fuss, any adult that the parent wants to flatter. They are interrupted in activities that the adults see as "only playing" whenever the adult wants either their bodies in a different place or to clean the space occupied. When they explore the world they are frequently hauled back without explanation and interesting objects are torn from their grasp because they are either too valuable or dangerous.

Infant protest at some of this treatment is regarded as rebellion and even normally reasonable parents can turn purple with rage that their child is "defying" them. I remember one woman friend that I had always seen as sensible and reasonable, turning into a terrifying Medusa-like figure screaming at her lively, disobedient, three-year-old son, "I'll break your spirit!" Who knows what demons from her own childhood were unlocked in that encounter.

Children cared for by substitute parents in nursery-type groups can also suffer an erosion of their sense of personal power. There are seldom enough adults to cope with the varying demands and the energy of a group of very small children. Most activities may have to be carried out in routines and the "good" children are seen as those who do not protest. Going to the toilet for instance, turns from being another exciting opportunity to enjoy the sensation of and exert power over one's own body, into a mechanical trick to be completed as fast as possible. So too in the nursery setting with eating meals and putting on coats. Speed in response demands a passivity, that allows you to be tugged and pulled and wiped when those in authority decide that's necessary.

With this emphasis on children doing as they are told, with messages that children have no power to question parental or indeed any adult decisions, it is perhaps hardly surprising that children do not protest when sexually abused. This is especially true for girls. There may be some recognition of a boy's need for autonomy but girls are often doomed to be powerless from the moment someone looks between their legs and sees no penis.

Going to school, all these lessons are reinforced. The ideal image is of the nice, polite child whose behaviour is always predictable, no tears, no tantrums, no fuss. Children are trained for an urban adult world that demands obedience and conformity. Queue here for a train ticket, queue there for the train. Don't protest if you're pushed and shoved, don't protest if your boss shouts at you. Don't protest if you're made redundant, queue quietly for dole money. Don't protest if you become ill and don't protest waiting for hours in a hospital outpatient department.

As adults we face lots of other demanding and even disastrous situations over which we feel powerless—death, disease, disability, famine or earthquake. Others are socially determined disasters—poverty, bad housing, unemployment. But people's reactions vary widely. Some of us cave in when faced with demanding circumstances. Others not only survive but triumph. Out of the disaster they find a new serenity and capacity to cope. Even those who have in the past appeared totally defeated can surprise us with new found strength in the face of adversity. They can face death and disaster with serenity, courage and humour. Others can go even further and add resolution and determination to change and improve a society that brings pain and injustice to its citizens. Why should this be?

Total acceptance of one's powerlessness is very rare. It usually leads to death. Holding onto some power to make decisions is necessary if we are to function at the simplest level. Those who appear passive and submissive do in fact frequently use techniques of manipulation or some means of covert delinquency to keep some sense of control over their lives. These are used in all kinds of ways everyday.

If a situation is too dangerous covert anger comes out in the form of delinquency and trickery. Some delinquency can be destructive when used randomly against fellow sufferers, but even that can keep the energy of anger burning. Trickery can be more creative as when concentration camp prisoners trapped the lice from the corpses of people who had died of typhus and inserted them into the newly-laundered shirt collars of the SS officers.

At the extreme of behaviour, sadistic and violent murder is a response, such as exercised by people like Denis Nilson or Charles Manson, by those who have had no outlets for this human need to have a sense of power.

But barring such gross and unusual exceptions, the most destructive effects of powerlessness lie in the everyday lives of ordinary men and women. An upbringing that insensitively limits their sense of power, inevitably limits their ability to own the power of their own feelings. If their infant expressions of tears, anger and rage have consistently met with no positive response, it will be given up in exhaustion and replaced with hopeless whimpering. If their toddler tantrums are suppressed in ways that teach that not just the tantrum but the whole child is unacceptable, the capacity to disagree strongly will be damaged. And since the confidence to express one feeling is undermined, the willingness to use any feelings can be threatened. So just as the expression of anger is taught to be avoided, the spontaneous expression of love or energy is also placed under a personal veto.

Those who crumble most severely under pressure may

be those whose personal history as children is not only of their own sense of self-determination being consistently thwarted, but who saw their parents as equally powerless to help themselves. This is why a sense of powerlessness is especially destructive in communities devastated by unemployment or poverty. Any social worker or health visitor making calls in such communities will see small children clustering fearfully behind their mother as she answers the door suspiciously, not sure if the person knocking is a friend or an enemy. Such children live in an atmosphere that lacks safety or confidence that the external world is one that they can control or influence. If school trips are arranged, the parents are powerless to find the money to pay for them. Opportunities for higher education for a bright child represent a threat to a fragile economy and have to be rejected. Where better-off children can persuade their mothers to buy them something, in poor families "good" children learn not to ask.

But it is not only the children of the poor who suffer an erosion of their power. Successful working-class and middle class families have more choice in financial matters and that is an important part of a sense of control. But if they are insecure in their social status, they can be so restrictive of their children for fear they step off the proven path to worldly success, that they destroy their children's confidence in their own intuitions and feelings. They build a protective box around their imaginations so that any ideas different from the proven way are not allowed to penetrate.

Identification with our parents and then changing to

become a person in our own right are processes that have to be faced at some stage in life. They are universal and timeless. On one level whether explicit or played down, our parents drive a bargain with us. Put crudely, it goes something like this . . . "Become what we want you to become and we will feed you, protect you , love you. Defy us and we will punish you and withdraw our love. There will be no compromise. Not only must you do what we want you to do but you must love us for making you do what you don't want to. You must also believe that we are right to punish you."

And generally at some level or other, we do believe them. In a culture where the rewards for adherence to parental values are all too clear and concrete, the penalties for rebellion can be dire. Built into the whole web of family and social relationships is the expectation that really, if we've any sense, we'll do what we're told.

However, in reality no one can ever be totally what their parents expect. In adult life when things go wrong it is easy to move back into a childlike feeling that it was our own fault and that we have failed to live up to the expectations of those in authority. Such people have no resources to fall back on and feel depressed and helpless. Nor are they equipped to resist oppression from those they should see as equals—schoolmates, colleagues or neighbours.

If at the same time, other voices reinforce those self-perceptions—voices of social prejudice which say things like, "Anyone can get a job", or "Women are stupid", or "Everyone on the dole is a scrounger", the identification with the oppressor is complete. It is the right to protest, to question, to challenge that has been denied. The early cry of protest has been smothered and not developed into curiosity, questioning and the ability to find alternative solutions to problems. If it survives at all, it shows in the corrupted form of attacks on those who are considered weaker.

Middle class and especially children of well-to-do parents have a decided advantage. They may have had to mute their protests in infancy and early childhood, but in adult life their environment allows them more chances for intellectual deviancy and eccentricity. The poet Edith Sitwell describes in her autobiography the desperate pain of her childhood. To her beautiful mother and aristocratic father she was not only the wrong sex but ugly as well. Her good intelligence was not welcomed. Governesses tried to fit her into a mould acceptable to her parents, physically as well as mentally. She was even strapped into a painful harness to improve her posture. But her parents' wealth made it possible for her to escape from them and lead her own life in London. She had been brought up in a beautiful physical environment which had enriched her imagination and through her more favoured brothers she had access to people and places who gave her the support and respect she had been denied in her own family.

The capacity to protest openly only survives if it brings results. It is helped by seeing that the adults around you have power. The need for power in our lives is so strong that even in the face of a steady build-up of eroding experiences, it dies very slowly. Each step in the loss of power is an experience of distress, an accumulation of hurts. This produces an apathy and an acceptance of further humiliations. It is the fear of reactivating hurt and humiliation that makes adults shrug their shoulders and say things like, "You can't beat the system", "Life is simpler if you just keep your head down and do what you're told", or the rhetorical, "What can I do?" The anger that would be the normal response to rejection, along with shouts of protest and tears of frustration has been buried, unable to survive being ignored.

We have seen how much easier life is for the parents of powerless unprotesting children. Life is also easier for teachers who have unprotesting pupils, jailers who have unprotesting prisoners, employers with an unprotesting workforce. Many men prefer powerless women in homes and offices. Our knowledge of the sexual abuse of children only makes sense if we recognise the power of men and the trained powerlessness of the children whose bodies they use. Residential care for people who are elderly is too often a battleground where the residents struggle to retain some power over their lives against the wishes of the staff to run a "tidy" and trouble-free establishment.

Yet any institution or group or society that contains a large proportion of powerless people is not a healthy society. A society that tries to keep the lid on protest and the human need for autonomy relies on people being apathetic. In terms of vigour and energy and the questioning of directions and values, a society that does not foster participation and empowerment, may appear calm but is in reality static.

So how can people be encouraged to feel in touch with a sense of their own power? How can we as a society share power energetically among many as opposed to retain it statically in the hands of a few? For those of us who have buried our tears, how can we move from apathy to creativity, from a painful spiritual existence to a vibrant and engaged form of life?

Much of the thrust of this book points to the view that as well as being tied into our political institutions, individuals' sense of self belief is formed first in the womb. The circumstances and the well-being of mothers-to-be and fathers-to-be are paramount. After baby arrives, the ways that she is cared for physically and emotionally takes primary position in influencing future health and vitality. Medical, social, financial, employment, housing and educational opportunities are of such necessity that they hardly need mentioning. But increasingly our society seems to discard its responsibility for these basic services. And the ways that parents and carers and teachers and grandparents and aunts and uncles and policemen and shopkeepers relate to young children and value them have been shown to be influential in encouraging self-belief leading to belief in and value for others.

At one time I made a study of how some children from very deprived backgrounds had been successful in doing well in later life. I identified three factors which seemed to be significant. The first, surprisingly, was illegitimacy. Many public figures like Ramsay MacDonald, the first Labour prime minister, have been illegitimate. It seemed that if a child does not know one parent it is possible to create a fantasy parent who can embody the child's aspirations and dreams. Such thoughts can liberate a child from the reality of the present and convey ideas of alternative ways of living.

The second factor was to have an adult in your life who gives you a sense of being special. This can be a parent but it can equally be a teacher, a social worker or a hospital nurse. Quite often it is a grandparent. I once heard, on the radio, the singer Frankie Vaughan who came from a Russian Jewish immigrant family being asked why he had chosen the name Vaughan for his professional life. He laughed and told the interviewer that when he was a small boy, his grandmother would say to him, "Frankie, you are my number *von*".

The third was to be found among children, living in an industrial society, whose family had originally come from the country and who either told stories about it or who might go back occasionally for a holiday. Sometimes the child was sent back alone for the summer. What seemed important here was that the child was given a sense that there were alternative ways of living. The idea that there is choice in life is central to the ability to grow and change.

But for those who feel the weight of life's demands or for whom a supportive enabling childhood is too late, what can be done? A look at some of the ways that people have succeeded can be instructive. In fact it never seems to be too late. The capacity to grow and change seems to be central to the human personality.

It very often takes some kind of trauma to shock people into a life change. A serious illness can make some people take stock of their lives. They begin to value and want to use more creatively the life that they feel has been given back to them. The death of a partner or a divorce, terrible though it may be at the time, can reopen for the survivor hopes and aspirations that became buried in the routine and compromise of a long marriage. Retirement kills some people but others use it to enter a third age of living and learning in which they can have more fun and satisfaction than they ever found in work.

One group of women who often find it difficult to claim their own lives are those who seem to be trapped in an abusive marriage. The central problem here is that they are subjected every day to treatment which leaches away any sense that they have power over their own lives. They are like hostage victims, constantly subjected to humiliation and feelings of helplessness. Many however, if they are offered opportunities to escape, will have the courage to do so. It is at this point that they need care and protection so that the small flower of their self respect can be nurtured.

Some women appear to fail and go back into the damaging relationship. They may feel that they are stronger now and can change the pattern of abuse. Some need to try several times before they are able to make a final break.

This is why it is so important to have refuges in which they feel safe and have opportunities to talk with others who have been through the same experiences and who can make them realise that what has happened is not their fault. The children of these relationships who come with their mother also need skilled help to change their image of a marriage if their own future is to be different.

Precedents, though painful and difficult, are encouraging. The average human being, no matter her apparent powerlessness, finds ways of fighting against helplessness. She knows that it she yields, apathy and death will follow.

This is clearly recorded in the history of prisoners of the Nazi concentration camps. I don't use the word "victims" because that signifies helplessness. The survivors of the camps did not see themselves as victims. Often those who did, died. Other former camp prisoners have described how they found different ways of holding onto a sense of power. Many of the studies of concentration camp experience show that it was the prisoners with a strong belief in the purpose of their lives who survived best.

Examples are political and religious prisoners in Russia both before and since the Revolution, in South America and South Africa. Political prisoners believe their imprisonment has some meaning—they are comforted by the belief that they have others behind them, even the forces of history are on their side. Prisoners held as a consequence of religious persecution believe that God is with them.

Different , yet as powerful, are the ways used to bolster an assaulted sense of personal power by those who have no political or religious faith. One friend of mine was brought up by her father in a way that encouraged her to have a strong sense of her own worth. In spite of terrible experiences of being separated from her family in a concentration camp, the humiliations of being stripped and shaved, the daily hardships and humiliations, she held onto a belief in herself. She held onto the the sense he had given her of her "specialness". Even though this drove fellow prisoners to nickname her "The Duchess", it was important for her to feel she had some sense of power over her captors, that she was not always subject to their decisions. One technique to achieve this was not to eat her bread ration at once but to divide it and eat the second half when *she* chose to, not when the authorities decided. This sense of being "special" was clearly an important factor in her survival, and contains a message for all parents who wish to give their children survival strengths.

Hope and anger can be very therapeutic. Again the extreme examples of the privations of war and imprisonment come to mind. A new inmate to a prisoner-of-war camp in Italy during the Second World War found his compatriots from a proud English regiment lying in their own urine and faeces, convinced that the Allies had lost. Still fresh and with confidence in the future, he shouted and screamed calling them cowards and scum until he aroused enough anger to start the slow process of clearing up their hut and rebuilding confidence.

Delinquency, trickery and humour are ways that a sense of power can be asserted in the face of what appear to be insuperable forces. The trickster figure in many ancient mythologies has pricked pomposity and high-handedness since the beginning of time. The capacity to laugh at a difficult and even threatening situation is a learned one. It may grow out of the humorous acceptance by parents that children will continually try to evade accepting authority. If the parents do not see that as a personal threat, if while staying firm, they acknowledge the skills exerted in for example, avoiding bed times, a child learns to value her capacity for creative challenge.

By using the experience of survivors, it is possible to build a catalogue of ways that personal power can be maintained and helplessness avoided even in intolerable situations. These include a sense of humour, curiosity, an awareness of injustice, faith in the future, and the feeling of being a "lucky" or "special" person. Central to all survival and creativity is the retention of the capacity to feel and express that feeling.

These are fragile capacities, perhaps developing late in the evolutionary scale. Our complex societies create so many threats to self-esteem, so we should aim to make it easier for fellow citizens to be protected from damaging experiences but also to resist and change them when they happen.

This can be done by first encouraging and applauding those who bring from their early experience those creative survival qualities we have identified. We all have a right to laugh at authority, to feel angry if insulted, to be horrified at cruelty to ourselves and others, to feel indignant at injustice and to weep for pain. It becomes possible for that anger, indignation and sorrow to be translated into thoughtful ways of overcoming their causes. We have to celebrate in our daily lives the capacity to show feeling and we can help young parents to respect their children's capacity to do the same.

Ways also need to be found of helping people whose capacities to feel have been blocked or distorted. Instead of expressing feelings and tackling the situations that give rise to them, they relapse into denial, become passive, identify with their oppressors and blame themselves.

The truth is that the core of caring about other people has to be the will to care about one's self. That for some people is difficult. Many can feel pain and outrage for others—we must be able to feel it for ourselves. Unable to care for ourselves, unable to feel our own pain, we are unable to care for anyone else. This is the ultimate damage of an uncared-for childhood.

It is when hope is thwarted that feelings like anger become destructive. We see this in rioting in areas of deprivation, which when put down by the police drives the community back into covert anger. And this often takes the form of delinquency that damages fellow citizens. Many simply return to apathy, a course that suits the holders of power.

Yet individuals, groups and communities do have at some time to take responsibility themselves for converting their covert or destructive energy into open creative protest. Some exceptional people can do this on their own. But most of us need the support of others. We can take our pain out into the world and ask those who also suffer to join us in transforming it. The very act of sharing pain, of weeping together, can bring a shift of energy.

Sharing the struggle is all-important. Recognising that we are not alone in our suffering gives dignity, sharing our tears validates them and gives the right to protest. As individuals and in groups we recover the right to state our view of the world, a right that was taken away from so many of us as children. We regain the ability to deal with authority figures without fearing that we will be made fools of. We can express what we think and feel without fear of being made to feel ashamed. We can practise protest against cruelty and injustice without embarrassment.

Individuals, groups and governments round the world and throughout history have indulged in all kinds of terror and oppression in the exercise of power. Normally though, they use a barely conspicuous and fragile web of control that first winds round us in childhood. It is a web of shame, embarrassment and uneasy guilt that controls us as surely as it did our parents. It's a web that discourages curiosity and assertion. It's a web that encourages people to take the easy way out rather than to confront issues head on. It holds us in ways that leave decisions to others, persuades us to respect authority without questioning its provenance. It chokes us if we seek to explore feelings that lie behind the face we learn to turn to the world. It inhibits the energy that makes us want to change the world and makes us say, "What's the point? Nothing I do will make any difference."

By understanding these patterns of restriction and ways of overcoming them we can enable ourselves and others, groups and communities to claim a fair share of power. In a world that increasingly emphasises conformity in all but the most trivial issues, the preservation and nurturance of creative protest is crucial for all our futures.

chapter sixteen
What to do?

At the beginning of our lives we only have needs. Wanting something comes later when we begin to develop a sense of ourselves as a person with a separate identity. The infant's hungers for food, comfort and stimulation are needs which if not met will stunt the body's growth and the development of the mind and personality. The cry which makes these needs known is a survival technique developed as part of being human.

In very poor and undeveloped societies there can be a conflict of needs between infants and adults. When it happens that there is not enough food to go round infants may be allowed to die. But in affluent societies there is seldom a conflict of needs between child and parent but there may well be a conflict between the needs of the child and the wants of the parent. It is here that the dilemma lies.

If a child's need is given priority by a carer, help or comfort will be offered immediately. There would be a search for the cause of the problem and an attempt to remedy it. Some mothers can recognise differences in the sound of the cry which tells them whether the need is for food, physical comfort or attention. It is thought that a prompt response to these needs actually reduces the total amount of crying an infant does in its first year of life. These babies also show better communication skills between eight and twelve months.

Mothers who persistently ignore crying during the first months tend to have babies who cry increasingly over the remainder of the first year. As you would guess babies who are talked to, smiled at and soothed while being fed and changed tend to be more relaxed. Non verbal messages passing between the bodies of the infant and the carer are of great significance.

If crying continues when the cause has passed it can often be stopped by distracting the child with sharp sounds or a visual image. Today's babies are being soothed with a recording of their mother's heart beats to which they became accustomed in the womb. Pregnant women who rested daily while watching the t.v. soap *Neighbours* often find the signature tune immediately calms their infant. A particularly effective way of calming a screaming infant is to massage its feet. Standing or walking about with the child is also more soothing than sitting since it more reflects the womb experience. Some mothers, during the first months of life, carry the infant constantly in a sling which keeps their bodies close together.

But it would be unrealistic to think that all parents or carers can offer this quality of care. A particular problem exists for that group of parents, ordinary, potentially loving, who have children who cry constantly and unremittingly. In the first weeks of life crying scores for babies range from 10 to 190 minutes a day. Caring for an excessively crying baby has been compared to sleep deprivation torture, and while the problem lasts the parents can take little pleasure in the child. This is really a conflict of needs with the child needing attention and the carer needing sleep.

Parents may live in a haze of exhaustion, anger and guilt, sometimes fearful of harming this child they wanted to love. Their own relationship may be strained to breaking point.

They can be left with a sense of failure for the rest of their lives. It is very important that these parents should seek outside help. There are now groups like CRY-SIS which give support and share helpful information. There are books written to help parents who want to understand what might have caused this problem but it has to be said that no one seems yet to fully understand why this cycle of tension emerges. Possibilities range from nutritional causes to the technological styles of hospital management of birth.

But part of the strain of parenthood is caused by the unrealistic expectations of what life with babies is like. The child is expected to fit smoothly into the life style of the parents where evenings and weekends are times of relaxation. Some husbands find it difficult to cope with their wife changing into someone else's mother and want nothing to change. But babies have their own timetable and may not be willing to be "put down" at seven and stay quiet till morning. The solution of letting the baby stay up until the parents go to bed or of letting the baby sleep with the parents may be more sensible. It's what happens in the vast majority of families across the globe.

In the industrial world, particularly in recent years, we have taken on a set of values which often have little to do with the inner life and needs of human beings living in the family and the community. Babies constantly remind us, if we let them, of fundamental truths about the human condition. One of these is the energy that lies behind tears. When they cry, their cry is a demand for change. They want life to be better. That is something we should all learn from them.

We now have much evidence to show that the force behind our tears, our emotional pain, is a powerful source of energy. We know that if we do not take it out and use it we can become tense and illness may follow. Or we can turn it against the world and use it to hurt other people. We can humiliate our partners because our parents never honoured us, we can abuse our children as we were abused. We can join groups which feed our anger and act it out in racist attacks or mindless terrorism.

Equally that energy can be used creatively. We can determine to create a world that will be better for our children than it has been for us. The energy behind tears helps us respond to and respect the needs of our own children. It can also help us extend tenderness and compassion so that we respond to the needs not only of those to whom we are bound in ties of family but to strangers. Out of this energy have grown the great humanitarian movements of world civilization.

But we have to start with our own needs. If we do not respect, love and care for ourselves we cannot respect, love or care for anyone else, including our children. Some of the experiences we have had in our lives may have damaged our capacities but it is important to remember that the very fact that we are alive means that someone, somewhere, at some time loved us. The wholly unloved child dies. That is a core on which we can all build to improve the quality of our lives.

Each of us carries within us a wounded child. It is in the nature of life. The only difference between us is the age at which we were forced out of the paradise.

The first commitment we need to make is to respect the child within ourselves. We can enter into a dialogue with that child, and in trying to communicate with the little one who was ignored or scolded for crying, recognise that we were entitled to cry. We were entitled also to be comforted.

This feeling that we were entitled to comfort may bring a stirring of anger against the parent who failed us. We may also have been taught that such a feeling is shameful or dangerous. But it is neither—it is normal.

Only when we can realise that no parent is perfect can we ourselves be fully adult. Most parents do some things well and some things badly. We can learn to be grateful for what they did well and forgive them for what they did badly. But forgiveness can only be fully given if we acknowledge the pain we were caused. With forgiveness comes the possibility of a love based on reality, not fantasy.

This opens the way to loving and respecting the child we were, and the person we are now. It is this child's memories, allied to our adult strengths, with which we work when we're trying to heal ourselves.

Some people prefer to work on their own to heal themselves and develop their capacity to live well. There are ways in which this can be done but it is not easy. Most of us need a companion, guide or friend who will walk with us through the dark places until we have the confidence to travel on by ourselves.

These are some of the basic assumptions on which all healing work is based.

For those who wish to work by themselves to move out of constant grieving and a sense of helplessness in the face of life's difficulties the first thing to which they have to attend is the state of their health. Many people who are sad and depressed eat badly. They may eat too little or too much and they rarely eat a balanced diet which gives their bodies proper nourishment. This is particularly the case for those who live alone. Because they have lost any sense of their own value they treat the body without respect as if it is something they simply have to drag around with them.

It takes courage to start eating properly. Even if you

don't believe it you can pretend that your body is worth caring for. You can stop shoving into your mouth anything that will take away hunger pangs and begin to think about the quality of what you eat. Tins and packets of food are often full of preservatives and sugar which may seem to comfort you but don't do you any good at all. Fresh food that you cook for yourself is much better. At this stage it is also helpful to take a mineral and vitamin supplement. In grief Vitamin C seems particularly helpful to many.

In the short term, it may help to take long, relaxing baths, read escapist novels, try aromatherapy or reflexology. These will help you to survive. But life ought to be about more than survival. It can be about joyous participation even while recognising the sorrows of the world. But this takes courage.

Don't get irritated if I say exercise is important—but it is, tremendously so. I'm not talking about violent exercises whose aim is to help you to lose weight but about gentle movements of your body to remind you that it belongs to you. It is also helpful to walk outside, in the fresh air. Gentle movements of your body are best done in the morning after you wash or take a shower. Try if you can to take a bath or a shower every day. Feeling fresh and clean also helps you to feel better about yourself.

Here are two exercises, one physical, one mental that you can try doing on your own.

Stand comfortably with legs apart.

First roll your head round your neck to the left, four times.

Then roll your head round to the right four times.

Roll your left shoulder round in its socket four times to the back and four times to the front.

Roll your right shoulder round in its socket four times to the back and four times to the front.

Let your arms hang loose then swing them as if they were limp ropes round your body as far as they will go, four times to the left and four times to the right.

Pretend you're a belly dancer and rotate your hips, letting your belly hang out, four times to the left and four times to the right.

Stand comfortably then bend your knees and rotate them together four times to the left and four times to the right. You may need to hold on to something to keep your balance for this one.

Last of all.

Lift your left leg and rotate the ankle four times to the left and four times to the right.

Lift your right leg and rotate the ankle four times to the left and four time to the right.

Try to breathe gently and deep into your stomach while doing these movements.

Don't worry if you feel too tired to go through the whole sequence. Just do what you can each day and you'll be surprised how soon you're doing it all. When you reach that stage you may want to do it twice or even three times. But always remember to treat yourself gently.

The mental exercise is for you to use when you're having a shower or a bath. If you're having a bath take into the bathroom with you a jug or basin. When standing under the stream of water or lying in the bath take three deep breaths. Allow the air to go right down into your belly and blow it out through your mouth. Then use your hands to soap your body and imagine that you are washing away all your resentments. As you rinse yourself off imagine all these negative feelings going down the drain. If you're in the bath pull out the plug and watch the soapy water running down the drain taking your resentment away with it. Then rinse yourself off with a jug or basin full of clear water.

It is very helpful to take some time every day to be quiet by yourself. If you live alone that seems like taking coals to Newcastle but it's not really like that. People who live alone often have their heads full of confused thoughts and repetitive phrases. Because they have no one with whom to share their angers, disappointments and irritations, the words they would have used keep coming back to them. The purpose of being quiet by yourself is to get a rest from these noises and give yourself an opportunity to let go of stress. Some people call this meditating.

It is now well known that taking 15 minutes once or twice

a day in this way can help many physical conditions like high blood pressure or emotional states like anxiety. The procedure is quite simple.

Find a quiet place. If you live in a house which gives you no privacy go into the lavatory and lock the door. Sit down as comfortably as you can but try to keep your spine reasonably straight. Take a deep breath down into your belly, hold it in briefly then let it all out through your mouth. Push out every last drop of tired old air from your lungs then start breathing normally but try with each breath to take it down into your belly and let your belly go all soft and relaxed.

Now all you need do is observe your breath moving in and out of your body. It may help to count the number of breaths up to five then start again. Your attention will wander, thoughts will come into your head. When you realise what has happened don't let that bother you. Let the thought go and start back counting your breaths from one to five. It's a help if you have a watch alarm or a kitchen timer that will let you know when time is up.

The first time you try this you'll be shocked at how difficult it is to keep your attention focussed but that will soon improve. If you can do this twice a day you'll quickly begin to feel the benefits. You don't need to sit for meditation. If it's more comfortable you can lie down with a cushion under your head and one under your knees to take the strain off your back. The difficulty about this is that you're likely to fall asleep. You can also use this breathing when sitting on a bus or train, or when you're out walking by yourself and do a walking meditation. But it's not sensible to do this in a busy part of town where you have to be alert for traffic.

Some people might prefer to meditate listening to music allowing the music to penetrate their minds and bodies. This has been described as dissolving into the music. For a sitting meditation classical music seems to be most popular, particularly Mozart, Bach, Beethoven and Mahler, but there is no reason that any popular music should not be used as long as it doesn't have distracting words. Everyone has their own favourite composers.

Some people meditate by humming. This is part of some ancient religious practices and is not humming a song but making a droning sound with the lips closed. It is thought to cause deep level relaxation and just as in the music meditation the humming becomes a space in which you can let yourself go and surrender yourself. Again you sit comfortably, close your eyes and begin gently to hum.

As you hum let the breath fall from you. Don't force anything and don't breathe out longer than feels comfortable. Let the sound do what it wants and as you exhale let the sound sink into the lower belly. If you feel tension there let it relax. Humming can be both a way of releasing anxiety and of gaining energy.

These are some simple ways of meditating. If you want to take it farther there are lots of good books which can advise you how to do that but using these simple techniques may be enough. But please don't forget that one of the most healing of all activities is laughter. It has been said that laughter is the highest form of meditation. As you read this you may feel that you will never again feel like laughing, but that is not true. Laughter is as important a part of our lives as tears or anger. It has powerful healing effects on our bodies as well as on our spirits.

Seek opportunities for laughter by watching good quality comedy sit-coms or comedians on television, look out for reviews of funny films and go to see them, read cartoon books like Calvin and Hobbes. Most of all try to spend time with people who have a sense of humour and for a time avoid those who are constantly miserable. You will not be able to help them until you are feeling better yourself and their low spirits will simply drag you further down.

This does not mean that you should not join with people who have faced in their lives the same dilemmas and problem you have known. But you should not be joining with them so as to go on being miserable together. The point of sharing unhappiness together is to move beyond it. If you are still locked so deep in your feelings that you are not able to cry then you will find it equally hard to laugh. Watch out for feelings of sadness that might lead to tears and instead of pushing them down try going deeper into them. If you feel tears well up when you are meditating, particularly when you're listening to music, have the courage to let them come. There is nothing to be afraid of. Try to see them as a strength rather than a weakness.

If you feel you are crying too much, then the next time you start when you're alone, go to a mirror and watch yourself crying. The most helpful tears are those which are neither so overwhelming that you have no control over them nor so detached and cold that they seem detached from your feelings. Learning how to watch what you are feeling, whether it's tears or anger is very helpful but it should not prevent you staying in touch with those feelings. They along with love are the source of your energy.

All the forms of meditation I have described above, and others, can also be done in a group. Many people believe that a group of people working together creates an extra quality of energy that can be very healing. Groups work best when they have some experience in common. This can be either personal life experience or some kind of common hurt. Pain is the most usual binding mechanism that brings people together.

Regular meetings, either weekly or monthly, when they have a common focus can bring people very close together. It can be a group of parents who have lost a child by miscarriage or death. It can be parents of children born with a disability. It can be adults who have learned that they may be affected by a genetically transmitted disease.

Your doctor man be able to advise you what medical self-help groups are available in your area. You will also find a list of self-help organisations dealing with a wide variety of problems at your local library.

The first and most helpful experience is the sharing of pain. This is not a case of saying that it helps to know that someone is worse off than yourself. That doesn't really help anyone at a spiritual level.

What does help is to see one's own pain as part of the experience of being human. It becomes less automatic to say "Why me?", a question to which there is never a simple answer. Because those in the group will be at different stages of confronting their grief and pain, members will see that these feelings are not static, that there is movement and hope. Perhaps most important such a group can offer informed love and support at a time when it is natural to reject help from outsiders whom you feel can't possibly understand.

In the process of learning to trust each other you learn again to trust the world. This is not as easy as it seems. Moving from the depth of apathy, through depression to feeling once again part of the human race involves being able to show your rightful anger at what has happened to you. But many of us find it very difficult to show our anger because it was not allowed to us when we were children. We had to push it back. Our parents preferred us being reasonable and depressed to being angry.

Being together in a group can give us an opportunity to express that anger safely since others in the group will share it. The interesting thing about anger is that you don't get stuck in it if it is freely expressed. What you can get stuck in is grumbling or irritability, so a group that only grumbles or expresses irritation does not help anyone. If the group can accept an individual's anger with respect and understanding everyone benefits. Anger is cleansing and often leads to the wish to take constructive action.

If our anger is not accepted, if we are told to count our blessings or that there are people who are worse off, we will go back to being depressed and apathetic. Sometimes the anger is hiding tears and sometimes tears are hiding anger. It helps to explore both these ways of expressing feeling. At first it can be difficult to speak openly in a group of eight or ten people so an alternative is for the group to move their chairs so that members can work in pairs.

It is often helpful to have one more experienced group member who acts as a guide or helper. It is usually better not to use the word *leader* since this may give a impression that one member of the group is "better than" the others. There is no place for "better than" ideas in this kind of work. The guide or helper, who should if possible be a different one for each meeting, can keep a note of time and keep a general eye on what is happening as well as laying out a possible agenda for the session. It should always be the members who decide what they want to do.

A question can be offered to the group like, "Can you remember the first time you cried?"

This can then be discussed between the pairs, each one taking five minutes to tell their story. After this they can turn back into the main group and either tell their own story or ask their partner to tell their story for them. The next question, back in pairs, could be, "Can you remember your mother (or father) crying?" or "How did your mother (or father) react to your crying?" Again the partners should each take five minutes before turning again to the larger group.

Other questions to be gently explored are:
What is your first memory of being angry?
How did your parents react?
What happened when your parents were unhappy?
What happened when your parents were angry?
What kinds of things used to make you cry when you were a child?
What kinds of things used to make you angry when you were a child?

It is important that each person is listened to very intently and carefully. To be listened to is in itself a very healing experience. Not more than three questions should be explored in the one meeting. Thinking and talking in this way can be tiring. It is also important to close the meeting in a very positive way. There could be a rota of members who will be available by telephone to listen to any member who feels urgently that they need to communicate something they forgot to say at the group. This should be made clear before the meeting closes.

A loving atmosphere can be created by the group holding hands and each person given the opportunity to say something before they leave. The guide or helper might choose to play a piece of music or read a poem which would comfort or inspire the group. The music doesn't need to be solemn, it can be lively and energising. Some groups like to finish with a short meditation. Finally each person should be thanked for having come and having shared their thoughts and feelings. This is a good point at which to have a goodbye cup of tea. If there are no catering facilities in the meeting hall the regular attenders could bring flasks.

Such groups are usually short of funds and are unable to afford very comfortable meeting places. Even so the meeting place can be made more welcoming by someone bringing a few flowers and a cassette recorder to have some music playing as people arrive. Some groups like to have a candle which is lit at the beginning of the meeting and blown out to signal that the meeting is over. These small rituals can be very helpful in giving a sense of meaning to the work of the group.

So, to sum up, answers to the question, "What to do?" might run as follows.

Don't fear tears—the tears of others, especially those of children.

Respect tears.

Listen to what our own tears are saying.

Listen to what other people's tears are saying.

Look at people who are crying tears.

Look at people who are crying silently.

Read faces.

Hear the sorrows that lie behind words.

Honour distress.

Respect pain, both physical and emotional, in yourself and others.

Share your pain with others.

Share your tears with others.

Be cautious about tranquillisers and anti-depressants.

Be cautious with any drugs, including alcohol, that anaesthetise emotional pain.

Be cautious with any behaviour, getting your own back, gambling or falling in love again, that anaesthetises emotional pain.

Grieve for your pain with your whole heart, then let it go.

If the wound is one which will never heal, and there are some, don't try to cover up and deny it. Acknowledge it as part of your life to which you give respect and attention.

Postscript

The twentieth century, more than any other in human history, has brought us a terrifying awareness of the dark and evil capacities of human nature. It is not that people in the past did not behave in evil and destructive ways. We have always known that human beings could be wicked and cruel. But this century has seen unprecedented horrors.

The Turks killed two million Armenians. The Germans killed six million Jews and an unknown number of Poles and other nationals as well as gypsies, the mentally ill and physically disabled. The Russians killed fifteen million of their own people. The Americans napalmed Vietnamese villages. Today we are horrified by what is happening in Bosnia and Somalia.

None of these events are very different in quality from the most horrifying experiences of the Middle Ages—the Inquisition, the burning of witches, the rape and destruction of towns by soldiers. It is not essentially different from the genocide of the American Indians, the Maoris and the

Aboriginal peoples of Australasia, the massacre by British troops at Amritsar.

Modern technology like gas chambers and napalm added to the horror by increasing efficiency of these horrors but that was not the significant difference. What horrified us most was that we had the illusion in Europe, fed by the new scientific age of the Victorians, that we were becoming better people. With good drains and better education we believed there came good sense. With learning and culture, love of painting and music, it was thought, came emotional sensibility and decency.

It has been the realisation that rationality and reason have failed that shocked us. All human wickedness needs to have agents who deny the importance of feeling. To shovel people into the gas chambers, for troops in Vietnam or China to shoot down villagers or students, it is necessary not to be moved by tears. To walk past men and women sleeping in cardboard boxes you need to deny tears. To accept poverty and homelessness for women and their small children, to accept the daily humiliations and injustice we inflict on the unemployed, or the physically and emotionally disadvantaged in our society, you need to deny their tears . . . and always to deny your own.

To build a new motorway you have to think it doesn't matter to destroy the habitat of wild birds and animals and cause distress. In order to burn down trees you have to not care about the delicate ecostructure. In the name of progress power is given to people who take pleasure in not caring about people's tears. This is the politics of tears.

In order to get people to behave like this it is necessary to tell them that tears are stupid, tears are childish, tears are a sign of weakness, important people don't cry, clever people don't cry. Of course women cry but that just shows how weak—how womanly—it is to cry!

I have written about women and how they hold onto the capacity to weep. Yet still we seldom see women using that capacity to weep and to retain contact with their feelings taking the lead in protest about public pain. They use their capacities almost exclusively to express feelings about relationships, with lovers, with husbands with children.

Some weeping that takes place seems a waste of time and energy. Women, if they gave more dignity to themselves, would not so often cry the tears of the victim. As I was writing this I had a visit from a young, beautiful, weeping woman. Behind a veil of bright hair she was hiding a savage bruise and she showed me her ribs where she had been kicked. The man who had done this was emotionally inhibited, unable to deal with his own pain and determined to make her suffer to ease it for him. By now, even her capacity for duty, tenderness and belief that she is responsible for his unhappiness are wearing thin. My hope is that her need for love, unmet in early childhood, will not lead her into a similar trap with the next partner who appears to offer it. If she does not use her tears to grow, if she continues weeping helplessly without mobilising intelligence and capacity for action, that will happen.

But it is important that, even if for the wrong reasons, women retain the capacity to weep and teach men to do the same. Most have managed to avoid the sterile traps of cynicism, of denial, of detachment and the world needs their emotional freedom. What matters is not that we weep but what happens when the weeping stops.

On a scorchingly hot July day, two years after my visit to the Hong Kong refugee camp, a taxi set me down at a small Zen Buddhist temple on the outskirts of a village deep in the Japanese countryside. Visiting Japan on a work commitment, I had decided to explore the Naikan therapy—*nai* (inner) and *kan* (observation). It was possible to do a concentrated course in one week but I had no idea what would be involved.

The courtesy and love with which I was met by the Abbot of the temple, his wife and family and the monks overwhelmed me. Within ten minutes of arriving I realised that I must abandon myself to this experience, shed all expectations and drift like a leaf on the wind.

Within an hour I was installed behind folding screens in a corner of the small, beautiful temple, sitting cross-legged on a cushion, facing a blank screen, with a dawning awareness of the strict spiritual discipline surrounding me. This place in which my life would be concentrated for fourteen hours a day for the next week was called the *hoza*, a term used in Buddhism to describe a place where the Buddha, or God if one believes in God, would surround and see me. It was a private place for me and the Naikan that I was going to experience would also be private. I need only share with the monks who would care for me, what I wished to share.

My guide or *sensei* who settled me in had prepared a translation of the first questions I had to consider. I read that I had to examine myself in relation to my mother from the time I was born until I was six years of age. I had to contemplate what I had received from her, what I had given her and ways that I had troubled her. This seemed a simple task. What memories I had of those years were vividly clear.

Crying had not been allowed. "What have you got to cry about?" she would shout at me. "*I* am the one who has suffered." I suppose there was a time when I cried freely, not only with a sense of self-disgust. Perhaps when I was born, torn so roughly from my mother that the incision made by the surgeons to enable my father to penetrate her was torn more deeply into her flesh. I am sure she cried in rage and pain, and perhaps that first Sunday morning we sang a duet as I too cried. I never discovered the source of her rage, but I was often made to feel that I was the source of her pain.

She was twenty three when I was born and if the photographs tell the truth, as beautiful as a pre-Raphaelite painting. It was the colouring, my aunts who feared and envied her told me—the pale skin, the great mass of crinkly Titian hair, the sapphire blue eyes. They blamed that hair for her temper, those flashes of rage that left them stunned and shaken and were to do the same for me. They were afraid of her. I learned to be afraid *for* her.

She wanted me to be perfect—that's normal, isn't it? Or is it? Before I was born, she told me, she used to walk in

Glasgow's Queen's Park, thinking beautiful thoughts so that I would be beautiful.

My tears seemed to be a threat—dangerous. Perhaps they truly were in ways that I do not understand. I only know my father's response to me through the lens of my mother's stories. It may have been that he, whom she loved with a bizarre obsessional hatred, would flee from my sounds of distress as he fled from hers. So, to keep me quiet, she stuffed her nipple into my mouth until I gagged. She was still trying to get me to suck when I was six. She told me it was because she loved me, but I was an evil child who doubted that.

I had felt I was an evil child long before. Small, solemn and dark, by the time I was four and sent away to a convent school, I had given up hope. I had lost my father. I had lost my mother too when she left me with my grandmother. I had learned to love my grandmother but in the convent I had lost her too. Now I had no one.

I had known something was going to happen. For weeks my mother had trailed me round a succession of large buildings asking if they would keep me and explaining that she was unable to look after me. I don't remember the words but I remember the atmosphere. I remember my grandmother's helpless anger.

Suddenly her problem was solved and in a state of euphoria I was showered with new clothes—a navy nap coat, a black velour hat, gym tunic, underwear, long black woollen stockings. For the first time I saw the Liberty vests with which I was later to become so familiar as exercises for my paralysed fingers to button up. I didn't cry when I was left at the convent. Instead I wet the bed. Every night my body wept at the wrong end.

Neither did I cry during or after the only visit from my mother that I remember. I didn't do anything. We met in the convent parlour, a large stiff room with a waxed floor, plaster images of the Virgin Mary, St Theresa of Lisieux and paintings of saints in various poses of ecstasy. She was sitting on a hard chair when I was brought into the room by a nun.

Even my mother's capacity for dramatising and sentimentalising situations when she had an audience must have been defeated when she was presented with the small wooden creature that I had become. For the first time the power was mine, not hers. The nun withdrew to leave us alone together but I would not let my mother near me. We were each alone and not together. It was the beginning of the end of my childhood. The end itself came two years later when, at the age of six, I left the convent on a stretcher suffering from infantile paralysis.

In the interval, as I waited for my fate to come and meet me, I learned to sew a fine seam (ten hemming stitches to the inch), I learned to read and I learned that I was different from other children. They each had a father as well as a mother and none of them, apart from me, wet the bed. Every morning I woke to find my nightdress soaked from hem to shoulders. Mother Stanislaus scolded, mocked, derided me, threatened me with the cane . . . all to no avail. I continued to wet the bed every night.

Finally I was given the ultimate sanction. One morning I was not allowed to dress. While the other girls were washing at the basins from where in the distance you could see Ailsa Craig out in the Irish Sea, I had to sit on my bed. Then, when all were ready and the crocodile formed to walk from the dormitory through the school to the refectory, the cold, smelly, wet sheet was stripped from the bed, wrapped round me and I was made to walk carrying it, by myself, at the very end of the line, followed only by Mother Stanislaus. Once in the refectory, I was paraded around, then made to sit by myself and wait until everyone had eaten before being marched back, by myself, to the dormitory to wash and dress before going to the schoolroom. That night, as I slept, I wet the bed again. It was my second awareness of power.

Now, sitting in the *boza*, as I meditated on these first six years of my life, I felt myself flooded with bitterness. Perhaps here in this strange country, among people I had no connections with, I could, without feeling guilty, express my sense of having been betrayed from infancy. Perhaps too I could let go my painfully acquired skills of trying to make sense of everything, which seemed to make it impossible for me to blame anyone for anything.

With the aid of a dictionary I prepared my responses carefully. What had I received from my mother? I slowly and ruthlessly listed . . . anxiety, misery, loneliness, fear, grief, rage. It went on and on. What had I given her? Someone to love of course, it was obvious. But also a focus for her tempers and her dramas. Had I troubled her? I didn't think so. I had always been a good, obedient, submissive child.

When my *sensei* returned, I was ready, smiling. We each performed the ritual greeting of mutual respect and I began. But before the first sentence was finished, he stopped me. "This word," he said, "*anxiety*, what does it mean?" I was halted in mid-flight and turned to the dictionary. He checked the translation I offered in his and then shook his head. "Naikan," he said, "is not abstract. It is concrete. Let us take the first three years." He bowed ceremoniously and left me with my little house of cards demolished.

When he returned two hours later, I had prepared a list of concrete words that I saw as utterly boring and irrelevant to my condition. I would however, see this odd experience through. What had my mother given me? Food, warmth, clothes, shelter. What had I given her? Nothing of course. How could I? What trouble had I caused her? None really. Certainly I had been ill frequently, but most children get ill.

My list was accepted and we moved on to the next three years over the next two hours, and then again the following three years over the following two hours. For the next two days, interrupted only by meals, the temple prayers and a highly formal and ritualised interview with the abbot, my life focussed on these three questions. "What had my mother given me? What had I returned to her? And what trouble had I caused her?" I could vaguely discern that there were other people in hidden corners of the temple but the strict rules that I must not talk to anyone nor get up and walk around without a specific purpose kept them as shadowy figures from whom I heard only an occasional moan or the sound of weeping.

By the end of my second day in the temple my house of cards had not only collapsed in ruins, it was torn into tiny useless scraps. Gradually my perception of the world was shifting. Instead of seeing myself and my needs as the fulcrum of all meaning, I was beginning to build up a new picture of this twenty-three year old who had given birth to me. Under-educated (she had left school at eleven), beautiful, courageous, ambitious, she went through her life trapped in an emotional and self-destructive nightmare constantly running inside her head.

For the first time in my life I began to weep for her and her pain. I saw her life as central, rather than mine. I was no longer the misunderstood heroine of the most important story in the universe. I wept for twenty-four hours and intermittently for the following two days. Before long I was weeping for myself as well, for the pain of our joint lives, for the pain of existence and for her husband and my father, whom I had hardly known and whose time and place of death are still unknown to me. I had the most extraordinary feeling as if the inside of my head had tilted so that I saw my life from a different angle of vision.

That has never altered. In a temple on the other side of the world in the Japanese countryside, I finally separated myself out from my parents. I went through the same Naikan process for my father that I had done for my mother, and then with all the other significant people in my life. When we are hurt by someone we love it is as if we are caught on barbed wire. Each movement to release ourselves causes deeper and deeper pain as we make new wounds, reactivate those unhealed and reopen old scars. Naikan helped me to stop struggling and to see the unrepayable debt I owe both my parents for their gift to me of life, no matter what happened after that. Somehow the barbed wire has dissolved. I have learned to weep more easily with friends for joint pain but for my own I still seek privacy. I now do so without self-disgust or wishing I was dead.

The story is not yet finished. When young, I sought serenity and yearned for maturity. I thought that was how you left pain behind. Now I know that even if we could leave our own pain behind, we will still have to live with the pain of others, their hurts, their sorrows, their griefs. If we pretend those don't exist, we are dead somewhere inside ourselves. But equally if we do not recognise that these hurts, sorrows and griefs can become the source of courage, of humour and of a blazing, incandescent capacity to love and celebrate life we have missed the point and missed the opportunity of a lifetime.

Suggestions for further reading

M Davis, E Eshelman and M McKay *The Relaxation and Stress Reduction Workbook* (California: New Harbinger Publications)

G Edwards *Living Magically: A New vision of Reality* (London: Judy Piatkus 1992)

E Goldschmied *People Under Three: Young Children in Day Care* (London: Routledge to be published December, 1993)

J Harrison *Love Your Disease, It's Keeping You Healthy* (London: Angus and Robertson, 1984)

J Kirkland *Crying and Babies* (Beckenham: Croom Helm, 1985)

M Konner *The Tangled Wing* (Harmondsworth: Penguin, 1984)

J Liedloff *The Continuum Concept* (London:Penguin 1976)

A Cameron Macdonald *Could It Be Stress? — reflections on psychosomatic illness* (Argyll Publishing 1992)

Alice Miller *For Your Own Good: Hidden Cruelty in Child Rearing and The Roots of Violence* trans H and H Hannum (London: Faber and Faber 1983)

R Moss *How Shall I Live* (California: Celestial Arts 1985)

C Patel *Understanding Stress–Self Help and Relaxation* (Consumers' Association, 1992)

C Murray Parkes *Bereavement Studies of Grief in Adult Life* (London: The Tavistock Institute of Human Relations)

Directory of National Voluntary Orgnaisations for Scotland (SCVO, 1992)

Voluntary Agencies Directory (NCVO, 1993-4)

If your local bookshop is unable to order American books they can usually be ordered through the Compendium Bookshop, 234 Camden High Street, London, NW1.

Other books by Argyll Publishing

COULD IT BE STRESS? reflections on psychosomatic illness

CAMERON MACDONALD

192pp Demy size pbk

ISBN 1 874640 10 6 £6.95

First published **September 92**

Consultant physician, Cameron Macdonald calls on a working lifetime's experience of emotional factors in common health problems from asthma to ulcers. A bestseller.

". . . makes psychosomatic illness easily understandable"
The Scotsman

"He describes how, through understanding the interaction between mind and body, healing can take place. . . humane and wise." *The Herald*

MAGIC CHILD

Kit Basom

272pp 197 x 130mm pbk

ISBN 1 874640 15 7 £6.95

First published **November 92**

One woman's journey of discovery, pain and recovery. Despite its portrayal of twisted morality, abuse and anger, this book is a moving and artfully written personal saga, and an inspiring one. With this her first book, Kit Basom is gathering readers by the boxload. *Magic Child* shows her deep personal insight as a survivor. And she connects with the experience of other women and oppressed groups like American Indians with whom she has faced the monster.

LET THE PEOPLE SING! a story of Craigmillar

Helen Crummy

240pp Demy size photographs and illustrations pbk

ISBN 0 9518593 0 7 £6.95

First published **April 92**

A story from divided Britain of Helen Crummy, child then mother and activist on one of Scotland's most notorious and much maligned public housing schemes. How a community came to question and take charge of the forces that shape their lives.

"A marvellously eloquent hymn of hope."
Ruth Wishart

"A life-enhancing account of an almost miraculous story. . . reveals the other side of Edinburgh as the Festival City."
Richard Demarco

"A story of community action told by one of the pioneers."
David Donnison